MIRAVAL'S
SWEET&SAVORY
COOKING

ALSO BY MIRAVAL

Mindful Eating

Mindful Living Miraval

MIRAVAL'S®
SWEET&SAVORY
COOKING

JUSTIN CLINE MACY
and KIM MACY

HAY
HOUSE

HAY HOUSE, INC.

Carlsbad, California • New York City
London • Sydney • Johannesburg
Vancouver • Hong Kong • New Delhi

To all the chefs who have inspired and mentored me over the years—
those who, like Cary Neff, Steven Bernstein, and William Cole, showed me
what mindful cooking was all about.

And most of all, to my wife, Kim.
I couldn't have gotten here without your love and support.

— JUSTIN CLINE MACY

To my mother, Janice; my father, John; my daughter, Sinatra;
and my husband, Justin . . .
for your love and support through the years.

— KIM MACY

CONTENTS

A Note from the Owners, Steve and Jean Case

If you've had the opportunity to come visit us at Miraval Resort & Spa, it's likely that one of the many experiences you'll never forget is the opportunity to enjoy incredible, flavorful, and healthful cuisine, thanks to Executive Chef Justin Cline Macy and Pastry Chef Kim Macy. As part of our commitment to bringing the Miraval experience beyond the resort in Tucson, we're thrilled to introduce *Miraval's Sweet and Savory Cooking*, featuring recipes from our Miraval kitchens that are practical, easy to follow, and delicious.

Drawing from more than a decade at Miraval, the husband and wife team of Justin and Kim provide secret recipes and tips on cooking and stocking a healthy pantry that will help you bring the Miraval experience to your own kitchen. We hope that you enjoy these wonderful dishes, and thank you for allowing us to share our passion for mindful, imaginative cuisine with you!

Welcome from Michael Tompkins,

Chief Executive Officer, Miraval Resort & Spa

At Miraval, I am constantly reminded by guests through direct feedback and on our Guest Satisfaction Surveys that the main reason people return so often is because of our staff. Through our mindful guest-service training, we provide customer care that is thoughtful, personal, and genuine. The atmosphere of compassion and respect is a direct reflection that Miraval staff members love their jobs.

What do I mean by *mindfulness?* Mindfulness is an elevated awareness of our surroundings and ourselves. It's all about being in the present moment, with a purposeful consciousness of our personal choices, strengths, and potential. Mindfulness is empowerment. It's a heightening of energy that leads to a better, healthier life—a life in balance. This is a cornerstone of the Miraval philosophy, and we emphasize the delicate balance among the many elements that we seek in life: intensity and relaxation, action and stillness, exploring the world around us and our own inner selves. We seek and need both ends of the spectrum, but only when they are in balance will our lives be in harmony.

An important aspect of that balance is applying mindfulness to what and even how we eat. If *spa cuisine* is the art of simplifying our foods—using natural, low-fat ingredients with an emphasis on fresh fruits and vegetables, whole grains, and lean proteins—then *mindful eating* takes the approach a step further. It reacquaints us with hunger rather than allowing us to feed our emotions. The guiding principle of mindful eating is *choice*.

In the Miraval kitchens, our chefs bring mindfulness to the table, from the fresh, locally sourced ingredients they use to the way in which each dish is prepared. Creating award-winning food that is both healthy and flavorful, the culinary team is also keenly aware of maintaining just the right balance between sweet and savory.

You might even say that there's a sweet and savory balance between the chefs on a personal level, too. You see, Justin Cline Macy is Miraval's executive chef, and Kim Macy is the pastry chef—and they're husband and wife. A large part of their lives is spent together in the kitchen, creating delectable meals that our guests will not soon forget.

The pairing of entrées along with breads and desserts to complete a meal is a dance that only truly talented chefs can master. It's a balance of flavor, aroma, and visual grace that when done right enhances our lives as it fuels our bodies. The key ingredient in completing a culinary masterpiece is that the passion of the chef must show in what he or she creates. I assure you that Justin and Kim have a love for their food, our guests, and each other.

MEET MIRAVAL'S SWEET AND SAVORY CHEFS

I can clearly recall my first interactions with Justin. He had been at Miraval many years before my arrival in 2007, and I remember how impressed I was by such a young kitchen talent. Over the years, I've found his dishes to be creative and sophisticated; they push the boundaries of spa cuisine to spectacular new heights. I was most proud of my tenure here at Miraval the day I promoted him to executive chef, as Justin is an employee success story, having begun his career in the Miraval kitchens as a prep cook when he was just 17 years old. After having worked under every executive chef, Justin blended the talents of each of those mentors to perfection, along with his creative aptitude, to bring our guests unparalleled meals. His experience in the Miraval kitchens was grown from the soil up!

Miraval Pastry Chef Kim Macy is amazing to watch in the kitchen. With baking requiring just the right amount of specific measurements and cooking and cooling times, it's not an easy job even for the most patient chef. Nearly all of the chefs I've ever met prefer not to work directly in the desserts, breads, and pastry areas because of the strict attention to detail. Kim's challenging work is further demanding because of the limited use of fats and sugars in recipes to conform to spa cuisine. Since coming to Miraval, I've watched her become proficient and skilled in her creations, even discovering hidden gems that bakers would never think of for a low-fat ingredient substitute.

Both chefs are masters at making their sweet and savory creations lower in fat and calories yet so beautiful and delicious that guests don't even think about that aspect. The two chefs never consider their dishes to be "health food," but rather delicious food that is full of lively flavors and appealing textures—and packed with nutrition.

Each side of the kitchen has a special approach to making the food deliver on the Miraval promise, and once again, balance is key to that equation.

WHEN JUSTIN CREATES

For Justin, it's about balancing the fat that a dish really needs versus the fat that many chefs might use without thinking about it . . . fat that adds calories but not necessarily a lot of pleasure. Justin looks for ways to reduce added oil, for instance, such as substituting some thickened vegetable stock for part of the oil in a salad dressing. The lovely texture of the sauce stays the same, but the fat and calories are cut way down. He also pays attention to sourcing excellent ingredients. "If you start with a perfect steak," he says, "you can trim it so it's virtually fat free, and it will still be delicious because of the superior quality of the meat."

And what goes in the sauté pan—or what doesn't—makes a big difference, too. In a typical restaurant kitchen, food is cooked in a lot of oil, which is mostly just for the convenience of the chef so that the food doesn't stick and will develop a nice browned coloring. But at Miraval, Justin has learned that he can significantly cut back on the cooking oil—even to as low as a quarter of a teaspoon of oil, as long as the pan is hot and the ingredients are properly prepared. He knows how to develop the flavorful caramelized surface that brings savoriness to a dish and never worries about food sticking to his pans.

Justin is all about spontaneity. He's very controlled and disciplined in his management of the kitchen and the production of food for the many meals and special events at Miraval, but when it comes to creating new dishes, even he isn't sure where his ideas spring from: "It's very strange. I'll be all geared up to develop some new recipes, and then it just doesn't happen. I usually end up with a pile of chopped ingredients but nothing that I'm satisfied with." However, inspiration often strikes the chef when he least expects it: driving to work, standing in the grocery-store line, or just as he's falling asleep at night. "Many ideas come to mind right as I'm drifting off to sleep. I've learned to keep a pen and paper nearby so I can jot them down."

For Justin, insight comes not from reading other people's recipes, but from what he sees around him. He's a visual creator, and the shapes and colors of seasonal ingredients are the starting points for the savory dishes that eventually grace the plates at Miraval. His process is one of reacting and improvising. Kim says that this is one of the reasons she enjoys watching Justin create a dish. "He's adaptable. If it's not turning out as he expected, he just finds another way to make the dish delicious."

WHEN KIM CREATES

On the sweet side of the kitchen, when Kim develops a new recipe, her process is deliberate and thoughtful. Her inspiration comes from many sources—beautiful dishes she sees in professional pastry books, favorite traditional recipes, or the sight and fragrance of a flat of fresh berries that arrive at the kitchen door. She always has a fully formed idea when she starts to create. "I'm hardheaded about it, too," says Kim. "If the dish doesn't turn out the way I imagined it would, I get frustrated and will just start again from scratch."

The pastry chef's day starts very early. While Justin stays home until it's time to get their young daughter up and off to school—at which point he begins work at Miraval, a workday that usually lasts 12 or more hours—Kim is in the Miraval kitchen by 5 A.M., baking breakfast treats, mixing bread dough, and creating the myriad components that will later become the spectacular treats and desserts that the resort is known for. The quiet of the morning pastry kitchen suits her meticulous, focused work style.

Kim also focuses on discovering the ingredients that truly count. She's happy to use real butter, fresh cream, and chocolate. Miraval's philosophy isn't about denial or restriction; rather, it's about mindful choices. Kim chooses to use smaller amounts of rich ingredients and only where they really matter. In her crème brûlée, for example, she keeps the egg yolks in the recipe even though they're high in fat because they give the custard the rich, satiny texture she wants. But she saves on calories by using lower fat dairy ingredients instead of all heavy cream.

Because pastry is as much a science as it is an art, Kim needs to do a lot of experimenting when she creates something new. Through trial and error, she finds the balance in a dish where the flavor and beautiful appearance are the first things the diner perceives, and the healthy aspects seem more like a lovely bonus.

CHEFS JUSTIN AND KIM have achieved a wonderful balance, both in the food they create for Miraval guests and in the loving family life they've built together. And it probably works because Kim's a little bit sweet and Justin's, well, more savory. Their diverse skills and personalities fit, complementing each other beautifully both at home and the "office."

And despite their different styles, these talented chefs are almost always on the same page. They understand the importance of hard work, consistency, teamwork, and—most of all— exceeding guests' expectations. These are the values around which "sweet" and "savory" come together, and this balance is the basis of the book. Both sides of the Miraval kitchen, and of Justin and Kim's partnership, are presented for you, with each chef sharing favorite recipes, along with the tips and techniques that will allow you to make them yourself, creating a little bit of the Miraval experience in your own home.

The Best **EQUIPMENT** for Sweet and Savory Cooking

A surefire way to make yourself a better cook is to make sure you have the right equipment. Every recipe will be much easier to execute, and you'll have more chance of success when you're working with the right tools for the job.

But that doesn't mean you need expensive or elaborate gear. Many of our most reached-for items in our Miraval kitchens are simple hand tools and basic cookware that you can find in any good kitchen store.

Here is the equipment that we'd like to see in every home cook's kitchen.

BLENDER

A blender with a large container (two quarts) and a strong motor will effortlessly make smoothies, salad dressings, soups, and marinades. If you want to invest in a real workhorse, you might think of getting a Vitamix, which is our preferred blender, because of its power, ease of use, and durability.

COFFEE GRINDER

We use a small (one-cup) electric coffee grinder all the time in the Miraval kitchens to grind whole spices, such as black peppercorns, star anise, cumin and coriander seeds, and dried chilies. *Quick tip:* To eliminate the flavor of one spice before you grind the next one, grind a small handful of rice.

CUTTING BOARDS

There is a huge range of styles and materials to choose from, but the first thing to consider is the size of your cutting board. A small board is fine for slicing lemons or cutting a sandwich, but to do any serious cooking, in which you'll be cutting and chopping lots of vegetables, for example, you need a board that's generous enough to hold your ingredients without them tumbling all over the counter. Aim for a board that's at least 12 x 18 inches.

Plastic is a good material for an all-purpose board; it's easy to clean and inexpensive. Choose a thick one, however, so it doesn't warp from the heat of dishwashing. Wood cutting boards are classic and functional, but they need more maintenance; treat your wood board once a month with a mineral oil so that the wood stays soft and doesn't splinter. With any type of board, bacteria can lodge in deep cuts or scratches, so clean the boards carefully and discard them if they get too worn. *Quick tip:* To keep your cutting board rock-steady when you're working, spread a very lightly dampened dish towel on the counter and position your board on top.

DISPOSABLE VINYL OR NITRILE GLOVES

While disposable gloves seem like something for a food-service kitchen, not a home kitchen, they're terrific when you have to handle hot chilies; they're also great for working with strong-smelling ingredients, such as onions, or ingredients that stain, such as beets. You can buy these at any medical supply store and many grocery stores or pharmacies.

FINE MESH STRAINER

You should have a large fine mesh strainer of some kind for straining soups, sauces, custards, and purees. Choose from a regular rounded strainer or a conical chinois (sheen-wah) style. Make sure the strainer you choose has a hook as well as a handle so that you can set it on a bowl or pan for hands-free straining.

FISH SPATULA

A fish spatula is a very thin metal spatula, usually with some perforations in the blade to let grease and juices drip through. The thin but flexible blade slides easily underneath delicate fish or any other item that might threaten to stick to your pan.

FOOD PROCESSOR

Food processors are essential to many tasks, from chopping vegetables and aromatics such as garlic to making pesto sauce and pureeing tomatoes. A good food processor will have a strong but quiet motor, a pulse button in addition to an on/off switch, and a bowl large enough to handle whatever you are making—although the size for a nonprofessional processor is generally a one-quart capacity.

HAND TORCH

You'll probably only use this gadget for one dish, but it's totally indispensable if you want to make a good crème brûlée. You can buy these butane-powered torches at kitchenware shops for not a lot of money, and since they don't take up much space in your cupboard, it's totally worth it. You'll feel like a real pastry chef as you caramelize your sugar topping!

HANDHELD CITRUS JUICER OR CITRUS REAMER

This simple, inexpensive tool will help you squeeze every last drop of juice out of citrus fruit just as effectively as an electric juicer. And it's much easier to clean!

HEAT-RESISTANT SILICONE SPATULAS

These are the go-to hand tool in our kitchens; they're much more versatile than a wooden spoon and easier to clean. Silicone spatulas are great for mixing, cleaning out a mixing bowl, stirring risotto, or scrambling eggs. The best spatulas can handle heat up to 800°F and won't melt during cooking like regular rubber or plastic spatulas will. They also won't scratch nonstick pans.

HEAVY-DUTY METAL KITCHEN SPOONS

Have at least one solid and one perforated metal spoon on hand for stirring stocks, soups, pastas, and such. Make sure they have long handles to keep your hands away from hot liquids and steam.

KNIVES—HIGH QUALITY AND SHARP

You'll be able to accomplish any kitchen task if you have these three basic knives:

AN 8- OR 10-INCH CHEF'S KNIFE: This is the wedge-shaped knife that allows you to efficiently chop your ingredients as well as slice them. German brands, such as Wüsthof and Henckels, are well made, sturdy, and slightly hefty; Japanese brands, such as Mac, Shun, or Global, tend to be lighter weight but are also high quality.

A LONG SERRATED KNIFE: A good serrated knife comes in handy for more than cutting bread. Use this for slicing tomatoes and citrus and for peeling melons.

A 3-INCH PARING KNIFE: This will be your "utility" knife for quick cuts, small slicing, trimming vegetables, and so forth.

If you want to expand your knife collection, we'd suggest adding an Asian vegetable cleaver, also called a nakiri, which is lightweight and not as wide-bladed as a "butcher's" cleaver. A slicing knife is also handy; this is a very long, thin knife that is helpful for slicing large roasts, smoked salmon, terrines, and other food for which you want your blade to span the whole width so you don't have to "saw."

And don't think that all your knives must match. Pick the makes and models that feel the best in your hand and that fit your budget. The most important aspect to a knife is that it is sharp. Not only will you perform your tasks with more skill, but you're also less likely to cut yourself because you won't be trying to force the blade to do its job. You can sharpen your knives with a simple manual sharpener, an electric sharpener, or if you're feeling cheffy, by using a whetstone. But know that the "steel"—the long rod on a handle that often comes with knife sets—does *not* sharpen a dull knife. The steel simply refreshes the blade edge before you use it. Once a knife gets dull, you need to actually sharpen it again.

MANDOLINE OR V-SLICER

It is nearly impossible to cut vegetables and fruit into very thin, even slices just using a knife, even when your knife skills are good. Cutting something thinner than around a quarter inch requires a mandoline slicer. You can choose from a large stainless-steel model or smaller, much less expensive, plastic models, usually Japanese, also called v-slicers. Both styles have extremely sharp blades and should be used with a hand guard or a mesh safety glove.

MEASURING CUPS, SPOONS, AND LADLES

We prefer plastic measuring cups to glass or Pyrex because they don't chip as easily. However, plastic is not heatproof, so keep it away from the flames. Use metal or plastic measuring spoons, preferably ones with oval-shaped bowls so you can fit them into the mouth of small jars, such as spices or capers. *Quick tip:* Take your measuring spoons off the ring so that they are separate spoons. That way, you don't have to fumble with the whole bunch every time you want to use one. Store them upright in a small canister or cup for easy retrieval.

Ladles are great for not only serving purposes, but also for portion control. A 2-ounce and 4-ounce ladle will come in most handy.

METAL KITCHEN TONGS

Some chefs wish they had tongs surgically attached to their hands—we use these a lot! We suggest having two lengths of tongs on hand—something around 8 inches and 14 inches—both with scalloped edges. These are indispensable for turning hot foods on a grill or in a pan, and they're also great for tossing salads or dredging chicken breasts through flour without getting your hands messy.

MICROPLANE ZESTER

This tool began its life as a wood rasp, for use in woodworking, but in the last decade or so has crossed into the kitchen and has been a game changer! The very fine notches in the rasp allow you to effortlessly add a burst of flavor to your food by easily zesting citrus, fresh coconut, ginger root, hard cheeses, or fresh nutmeg or cinnamon into a dish. These zesters come in different sizes and shapes, each with a slightly different function, but the long narrow one with small holes is a good all-purpose model.

MIXING BOWLS

A set of mixing bowls in graduated sizes is invaluable (make sure they "nest" for easy storage). Ceramic can be pretty but is heavy and breakable. Glass allows for use in the microwave but has the same problems as ceramic. Stainless-steel bowls are incredibly versatile, and they're indestructible. You can find these bowls in a million sizes at all kitchenware stores and at very reasonable prices at your local restaurant-supply store.

MUFFIN TINS, BAKING PANS, AND SPRINGFORM PANS

Muffin tins can be useful for more than just muffins; they can also be used as molds for tuiles, crepes, or eggroll wrappers to create a bowl shape. You should also have an 8 x 8-inch and a 9 x 13-inch baking pan, either in metal or Pyrex. You'll need a springform pan for cheesecakes (and also for the Mixed Berry Torte).

OFFSET SPATULA

These simple metal spatulas, which have a 90-degree angle in the blade, are probably the most used utensil in our bakeshop. Offset spatulas are great for smoothing frosting on a cake, spreading tuile batter, and several other tasks. It's good to have several sizes on hand so that you use the right size for the job.

PASTRY BAG AND STAR TIP

A pastry bag, also called a piping bag, fitted with either a plain tip or a star tip can be helpful for filling pastries or making purees look good on the plate.

In a pinch, you can use a one-gallon heavy-duty plastic bag instead of a pastry bag. Spoon the ingredients into the bag, cut one corner with scissors, and then pipe out the ingredients.

PLASTIC SQUEEZE BOTTLE AND TIP

Squeeze bottles are great for "painting" plates with pureed sauces and reductions for a more attractive presentation. You can find these in most supermarkets, and the bright red and yellow ones made for condiments work just as well as the clear ones. Clean them well after each use.

PLASTIC TRIGGER SPRAY BOTTLE

At Miraval, we consider spray bottles to be the single most important kitchen tool to help reduce calories. We fill our bottles with Miraval Oil Blend and use them to lightly coat pans for sautéing foods, roasting vegetables, and more.

Each pull of the trigger should spray between an eighth and a quarter teaspoon of oil, allowing you to easily control the amount of fat (oil) you're using.

Trigger spray bottles can be found in supermarkets and home and garden stores. We like these simple bottles better than the aerosol-pump spray bottles (misters) sold in most kitchen-equipment stores. The trigger bottle releases the oil in droplets instead of in a mist, which cooks away quickly, and it won't clog. There's also no spring to break, unlike in aerosol-pump bottles. We do sometimes call for nonstick cooking spray, which is a ready-to-use product that is ideal for preparing pans for baking, for example, but we prefer to use the trigger spray bottle for sautéing and most other cooking needs.

POTS AND PANS

Good quality pots and pans are worth investing in. It's hard to cook well with inferior cookware, and once you've bought a good pan you'll have it for life.

What makes good cookware? All pots should have riveted metal handles and thick bottoms so they can go straight from the burner into the oven. A thick bottom is crucial for consistent temperature and even cooking and to prevent warping. Generally, stainless-steel-lined pans with an aluminum core (sometimes called three-ply) are the best all-around performers; they heat quickly and evenly and hold heat well. Other materials we like include enameled cast iron, such as Le Creuset or Staub, and traditional cast iron. An old-fashioned, cast-iron skillet is one pan that won't cost you a lot yet will provide a lifetime of good service.

Here's what we recommended in terms of sizes and styles:

8-INCH, 10-INCH, AND 12-INCH STAINLESS-STEEL SAUTÉ PANS OR SKILLETS

A 12-INCH CAST-IRON SKILLET

2-QUART, 3-QUART, AND 8-QUART SAUCEPANS

A LARGE STOCKPOT, at least 16-quart, which can double as a pasta pot

Additionally, a wok with a lid is handy and can be used as a steamer when fitted with a bamboo steamer insert. A heavy roasting pan can be used not only for roasting meat and poultry, but for roasting vegetables, too, and even for very large casseroles.

Finally, be sure to have two heavy-duty, rimmed, aluminum baking sheets, also called half sheet-pans.

A note on nonstick pans: At Miraval, we generally don't use nonstick pans because it's nearly impossible to achieve a good seared surface on our food. It's also very easy to compromise the coating, whether by heating to a very high temperature or by scratching with a metal utensil or a scrub pad. In either case, you could expose yourself and the environment to the toxic chemicals used to make the coating.

We do make an exception, however, for cooking eggs, which is difficult to do without a nonstick pan.

So if you're using nonstick, hand wash it with warm soapy water (dishwashing shortens its life), watch out for scratches, and don't overheat the pan.

SILICONE BAKING MAT

While these mats aren't inexpensive, they are an alternative to greasing or using parchment paper on a baking sheet, and ultimately, they will save you lots of time and trouble. They're completely nonstick, don't retain flavors, and are heat resistant to about 650°F. Each mat can be used thousands of times. Wash them well in warm soapy water after each use, allow them to air-dry, and store flat or rolled.

STAND MIXER

Advanced bakers and cooks may want to consider a stand mixer. KitchenAid is one of the best-known brands. Their mixers are used in many commercial kitchens, including ours. A KitchenAid mixer is an investment, but it will last for generations. It is so much easier to use than a handheld mixer, not simply because of its more powerful motor and good attachments, but because it leaves your hands free to add ingredients and such.

VEGETABLE PEELER

Whether you choose a straight-blade peeler, a swing blade (such as you'll find in a grocery store), or a Y-peeler is a matter of what feels right in your hand. Whichever model you choose, make sure it's well made so it will last you for years.

Kitchen **TIPS** and Helpful **HINTS**

VENTILATION

Make sure that your kitchen is properly ventilated with a hood or fan system. This will decrease any smoke during sautéing and minimize your risk of a potential fire.

OVEN MITTS OR TOWELS

As simple as it may seem, it's crucial to have dry, clean towels or oven mitts at your grasp. Never attempt to grab something out of the oven with a damp towel because the steam that's created can seriously burn you.

NONSLIP FLOORS OR MATS

Okay, we don't expect you to have your kitchen floor coated with a nonslip surface like a professional kitchen. However, a slick tile floor + food = an accident waiting to happen. So it's important to either wear slip-proof shoes or use kitchen mats, and always keep your floors clear of debris.

COLOR-CODED CUTTING BOARDS

Using color-coded cutting boards designated for different food types such as fish, poultry, vegetables/fruits, raw meat, and cooked meat can seriously reduce the risk of cross contamination between raw and cooked products. Several online sites now carry such cutting boards that will help keep you safe and free of food poisoning.

DISINFECTANT SPRAY

Have a disinfectant spray handy, especially when handling raw animal products.

USE HEAVY-DUTY KITCHEN EQUIPMENT

Nowadays many kitchen bowls and utensils are designed with one thing in mind: looks, not functionality. When picking out your kitchen utensils, it is important to think about how long they will last, as well as any safety issues. Having too many clay, glass, or ceramic utensils can be a hazard in the kitchen, especially because they break and chip easily. So when choosing these items, go for mostly stainless steel and aluminum.

KNIFE SAFETY

KEEP YOUR KNIVES SHARP: You're more likely to cut yourself with a dull knife than a sharp one. Using a dull knife requires more downward pressure to cut and could result in the blade slipping and cutting you. Use one of the many good sharpening tools on the market or a professional knife-sharpening service.

USE A KNIFE FOR ITS INTENDED PURPOSE: Never try to open a can or bottle with a knife or use a knife as a screwdriver. Don't use your knives to cut string, boxes, bones, metal, or paper, as these materials will dull your knife, put nicks in the blade, or even break it.

ALWAYS USE A CUTTING BOARD: Never cut something while holding it in your hand! Use a cutting board, and keep it in place on your work surface by placing a damp towel underneath it. This will keep the board from shifting or sliding while you use it. Make sure the board is on a flat surface, free of clutter, and big enough for the task at hand, which will allow you to work more efficiently.

CHOOSE THE CORRECT KNIFE: Use a paring knife for peeling fruits and vegetables, a chef's knife or Asian-style cleaver for chopping and mincing, a serrated knife for slicing, and so forth.

HAND WASH KNIVES IN HOT, SOAPY WATER: Never put knives in the dishwasher, as high heat and caustic detergents can corrode blades and swell handles over time. And don't put a knife into a sink filled with sudsy water—you could inadvertently cut yourself when you reach down to retrieve it.

ALWAYS HOLD A KNIFE BY ITS HANDLE: When cleaning, turn the blade away from your hand, and never run a cloth down its edge.

STORE KNIVES PROPERLY: A magnetic knife rack or knife block is best. If you are storing knives in a drawer, keep them in a separate compartment. Line the area with a rubber mat or towel to prevent the knives from sliding into each other when you open and close the drawer.

PAY ATTENTION: Keep your eyes on your cutting board, knife, your non-cutting hand, and whatever you're cutting or chopping. Don't allow yourself to be distracted by conversations, children, pets, or the television.

Always use caution. When chopping peppers, for instance, make sure that you've removed all the seeds from the cutting board, the pepper to be cut, your hands, and your knife. The slippery seeds often contribute to kitchen accidents involving knives.

And finally, if you drop a knife, ignore the instinct to catch it! Step back and wait until it comes to a complete rest before picking it up.

The Sweet and Savory Cooking
PANTRY

Every good cook knows that no matter how good a recipe is, if your ingredients aren't great, your final dish will always disappoint. That's why choosing the best and most appropriate ingredients is the first step in the cooking process. We try to choose the freshest produce at its peak season, and always organic and local, if possible.

The same goes for meat, poultry, and dairy products—we look for meat, eggs, and milk or cream that's produced from humanely raised animals. As for seafood, fish and shellfish are an extremely important part of Miraval menus because they are naturally low in fat and high in healthful omega-3s and other nutrients. We try to choose seafood that's from sustainable fisheries, caught using methods that preserve the integrity of the fish. And of course, freshness is paramount when it comes to seafood.

In this section, we'd like to highlight some ingredients that you should have in your pantry, both in order to make the recipes in this book and to allow you to create all sorts of healthful meals. We're focusing in particular on ingredients that you may not have heard of or about which you may have some questions.

BEANS AND LENTILS

These ingredients, also known as "pulses," are nutritional powerhouses, full of protein, vitamins, and fiber . . . and of course virtually no fat. Canned beans or chickpeas are perfectly fine and convenient, or you can cook the dried versions from scratch. Most beans benefit from an overnight soak before cooking, and you should always pick over your beans or lentils to look for tiny rocks, which have a way of sneaking in. The basic cooking method is to simmer them in nicely salted water until the beans are very tender. Let them cool in their cooking liquid to help them keep their shape. Lentils will cook much quicker than larger beans.

There are many interesting heirloom bean varieties on the market nowadays, so look for something you haven't tried, just for fun. Most bean types are interchangeable in recipes. For lentils, look for the green French lentils, which will hold their shape better than brown lentils.

NUTS AND SEEDS

These are full of healthful oils as well as fiber, and of course they provide delicious crunch to many dishes. Nuts also can be ground into a coarse meal or fine flour and used in baking and pastry to add not only nutrition, but also wonderful flavor. Almonds are most commonly used this way, but hazelnuts are excellent, too.

Even though you find these products in the dry-goods section of the store, nuts and seeds are very perishable, so be sure to store them properly. If you won't be using them within a week, you should store them, tightly sealed, in the freezer. Always taste your nuts or seeds before using to be sure they haven't gone rancid.

Our favorite nuts: Almonds, cashews, pecans, pine nuts, pistachios (shelled), walnuts

Our favorite seeds: Flax seeds, pumpkin seeds, sesame seeds (black and white), sunflower seeds

FLOURS AND MEALS

ALL-PURPOSE FLOUR: Choose unbleached flour, which has slightly more nutrients and protein.

ALMOND FLOUR: Extremely flavorful in cakes and pastries and will add a slightly coarse texture.

BROWN RICE FLOUR: Flour milled from the whole rice kernel; it's gluten-free and high in fiber, vitamins, and minerals.

CAKE FLOUR: Very finely milled wheat flour that has been bleached, which minimizes gluten and therefore toughness. Nutritionally, cake flour is pretty empty, but its use is appropriate in certain very delicate pastries and cakes.

CORN STARCH: Used for thickening mixtures.

GARBANZO (CHICKPEA) FLOUR: Highly nutritious, used in the cooking of South Asia, but strongly flavored, so it's not very versatile.

MASA (CORN FLOUR): This is the basis of tamales and other Mexican corn-based dishes. Masa is also a good thickener for stews and soups.

POTATO STARCH: Used as a thickener but also plays a role in gluten-free baking mixes.

TAPIOCA FLOUR: This is a starchy, slightly sweet, white flour made from the cassava root, so it is totally grain-free.

WHOLE-WHEAT FLOUR: This is wheat flour in which the outer bran and the inner germ are still intact, so you get the full nutritional value of the wheat. Whole-wheat flour has less protein by weight than all-purpose flour, and therefore baked goods and pastas made with all whole-wheat flour won't have the same springy texture as traditionally made dishes. Look also for white whole wheat, which is milled from hard white spring wheat, rather than traditional red wheat, and is lighter in color and sweeter. Check out whole-wheat pastry flour, too, which is milled from soft white wheat that gives it a low protein content; it is also called graham flour.

XANTHAN GUM: This is a natural carbohydrate that is milled into a powder and used in gluten-free cooking and baking to bind, thicken, and emulsify gluten-free ingredients.

SWEETENERS

All sweeteners are essentially the same, combinations of fructose and sucrose molecules, but each has a slightly different flavor profile; and some cooks prefer to cook with sweeteners that are less refined than regular granulated sugar. At Miraval, we choose the sweetener that's best for the recipe.

AGAVE SYRUP: A sweet syrup derived from the agave plant, which is the same plant from which tequila is produced. Agave syrup is sweeter than regular sugar, and therefore you can use less of it to achieve the same sweetness level.

BROWN SUGAR: Refined white sugar to which molasses has been added back to give a caramel flavor and moisture. There are also unrefined brown sugars such as turbinado (Sugar in the Raw) and muscovado, which is a very dark, unrefined brown sugar from the Caribbean with a strong molasses flavor.

POWDERED (CONFECTIONERS') SUGAR: Very finely ground granulated sugar used mostly for dusting. Cornstarch has been added to prevent clumping, so confectioners' sugar is not 100 percent sugar.

MOLASSES: A dark, thick syrup produced as a by-product of refining sugar cane or sugar beets into sugar.

UNREFINED CANE SUGAR: This is crystallized cane juice that has not undergone all the processing and bleaching that regular granulated sugar has. Chemically, it is the same substance as white sugar, but there are trace nutrients remaining in unrefined sugar.

CHOCOLATE AND COCOA

BAKER'S CHOCOLATE: This is 100 percent cocoa solids, meaning it is completely unsweetened. Used only in baking.

DARK CHOCOLATE (64 PERCENT OR HIGHER CACAO CONTENT): We used to see the terms "semisweet" and "bittersweet," but neither of these is defined by law and therefore are slightly meaningless in terms of letting you know how sweet the chocolate would be. "Dark" is a better term. There are many fine quality chocolates on the market now, ranging from around 55 to 80 percent cocoa solids, each with particular flavor profiles. Experiment to find what you like.

UNSWEETENED DARK BAKER'S COCOA POWDER (NOT DUTCH PROCESSED): Also called natural cocoa powder, this is the ground cocoa mass from chocolate, with most of the cocoa butter pressed out, though not all. Cocoa powder is wonderful in desserts because it can deliver a very full chocolate flavor without much fat.

DAIRY AND DAIRY SUBSTITUTES

ALMOND MILK: A beverage made from ground almonds that contains no dairy, cholesterol, or lactose.

BUTTERMILK (FAT-FREE): Despite the name, this is not buttery at all, but rather it's the whey that is left over after making butter. Most buttermilk is cultured, so it's thickened and has a distinct tang to it. Buttermilk is wonderful in cakes and pastries because it brings a subtle tangy flavor, and the high acid content creates a very tender crumb structure.

COCONUT MILK: Mostly available in cans. Note that the "cream" will float to the top of the can, so you need to stir to blend before you measure and use coconut milk.

EVAPORATED SKIM MILK: Adds rich flavor without the fat.

KEFIR: A cultured dairy product, much like a drinking yogurt. Kefir is full of healthful probiotics.

RICE MILK: A beverage made from brown rice that contains no dairy, cholesterol, or lactose; it can be naturally slightly sweet.

SKIM AND/OR 2 PERCENT MILK: Lower-fat alternatives to whole milk, which is generally 3.8 percent fat.

SOY MILK: A beverage made from soybeans; it contains no dairy, cholesterol, or lactose.

YOGURT (PLAIN): Available in full-fat, low-fat, and nonfat versions. Adds tang and moisture to baked goods and is wonderful in dips and sauces or as a condiment to spicy chilies, soups, and stews. Use plain yogurt in place of sour cream.

GRAINS

ARBORIO OR CARNAROLI RICE: A medium-grained Italian rice variety used for risotto. These rices give off a lot of starch when cooked, which creates risotto's characteristic creaminess.

BARLEY: Wonderful grain with a chewy, moist texture. Good in soups and stews because it doesn't become mushy.

BLACK FORBIDDEN RICE: Also called purple rice, black rice is high in nutritional value and contains 18 amino acids, minerals, and vitamins. Due to its dark color, which turns more purple when cooked, it is high in anthocyanins.

BROWN BASMATI RICE: The whole-grain version of the prized long-grained Indian rice. Fragrant and delicately chewy.

BULGUR: Cracked wheat, often used in Middle Eastern cooking. To prepare bulgur, you don't boil it like other grains; you soak it so it absorbs water and becomes tender.

KAMUT: A form of ancient wheat, related to durum wheat.

JASMINE RICE: An extremely fragrant rice used in Southeast Asian cooking; long grained and delicate.

BROWN RICE, LONG- OR SHORT-GRAIN: This is rice in its whole-grain form, complete with bran. Brown rice provides more fiber and nutrition than white rice. It takes longer to cook and is generally chewier and less fluffy than white rice, but it is delicious.

OATS, ROLLED AND STEEL-CUT: Rolled oats are the flat flakes that we're more used to for baking and breakfast cereal. They are fairly quick cooking. Steel-cut oats are oats that are not flattened but rather are chopped into tiny pellets. They are delicious as a hot cereal, but they take longer to cook.

POLENTA, QUICK-COOKING AND TRADITIONAL: This is cornmeal, Italian style, though polenta and American grits or cornmeal mush are very similar. All corn meals come in fine, medium, or coarser grinds; and for polenta or grits, you want a coarse grind. Quick-cooking polentas have been partially cooked, so they only take five minutes to become tender enough to eat, but they lack the satisfying mouthfeel of real, long-cooked polenta.

QUINOA: A grain-like seed that originated in the Andes region. Not a true grain, it is nonetheless extremely nutritious and easy to cook.

WHEAT BRAN: The outer layer of the wheat grain that's removed during milling. It is very high in fiber and can add texture and nutty crunch to dishes.

WILD RICE: This is technically not a rice but a grass seed, which grows in marshy areas of the U.S., especially in the Great Lakes regions. The grains are long and hard and require long simmering in water or stock, but once tender and popped open, they are delicious, chewy, and highly nutritious.

YELLOW AND BLUE CORNMEAL: A finer version of polenta used in baking or as a coating for baked or fried food. Blue cornmeal is ground from a blue variety of corn; the flavor is indistinguishable from yellow cornmeal.

OILS AND FATS

COLD-PRESSED CANOLA OIL: Canola is also called rapeseed oil; it is high in polyunsaturated fat, mild to neutral in flavor, and has a high smoke point, so it is a great oil for sautéing and frying. Cold-pressing means that the oil has been extracted only by pressing the seeds, not by extraction with solvents or heat; it's an indication of quality.

COLD-PRESSED EXTRA-VIRGIN OLIVE OIL: Extra-virgin means the oil has a low acid content, which indicates high quality, better flavor, and more nutritious polyphenols. All extra-virgin oils are cold-pressed, so this designation is somewhat redundant.

GRAPE-SEED OIL: This is a bright green oil with a nutty, pleasant flavor and a high smoke point. It is also lovely as a blending oil for salads and marinades.

NONSTICK COOKING SPRAY: Vegetable spray delivered from a can. We mostly use this to prepare baking pans and baking sheets so ingredients don't stick, but sometimes we'll grease a skillet with just a touch of fat from this spray.

SESAME OIL: We mostly use toasted sesame oil, which is darker in color, extremely flavorful and fragrant, and should only be used as a flavoring oil, not for cooking. Untoasted sesame oil is also available and is better suited for heating and cooking, but its flavor is fairly neutral.

UNSALTED BUTTER: We use unsalted butter in order to control the amount of salt that we use in our cooking. Keep butter tightly wrapped in the refrigerator so that it doesn't absorb odors.

VEGAN BUTTER: A spread made from nondairy ingredients, such as soy oil or nut oils.

COCONUT OIL: This is a no-cholesterol oil (no vegetable products contain cholesterol) that has a high smoke point and is resistant to turning rancid, so it has a long shelf life. Although it contains no cholesterol, it's higher in saturated fats than most vegetable oils.

WHITE TRUFFLE OIL: A special, intensely flavored and perfumed oil made from the essence of truffles. Be sure to choose oils that are made from all-natural ingredients rather than from synthetic truffle essence.

Sweet and Savory Cooking
SECRET INGREDIENTS

KIM'S SWEET SECRET INGREDIENT

FRESH SEASONAL BERRIES. They are so versatile; you can add them to anything. A little jumble of berries adds height, color, flavor, and, of course, minimal calories. Plus, loads of nutrients. My favorite are raspberries, for their gorgeous color, sweet perfume, and ease of use—no stems or big seeds to worry about. The perfect balance of so many good things!

JUSTIN'S SAVORY SECRET INGREDIENT

MIRAVAL'S BALSAMIC REDUCTION. Whenever a dish needs a little more punch, I drizzle on some of this sweet-tart vinegar reduction. Miraval guests frequently compliment us on this accent, asking whether I'm using 80-year-old artisanal balsamic.

The truth is that the vinegar isn't expensive; it's just carefully reduced to the right balance of sweet, savory, and sour. You can easily create this secret ingredient at home. (See page 119 for the recipe.)

Kim's
Breakfast Treats,
Quick Breads,
and Yeast Breads

FLUFFY GLUTEN-FREE PANCAKES

Having success with gluten-free recipes isn't just a matter of using the right ingredients; it's also about cooking things properly. You need to know that these pancakes don't behave quite the same as "traditional" ones—you won't see a lot of bubbles forming as you cook the first side, and you'll need to cook them a touch longer than you think you might. The best way to test is by taking a bite! **MAKES 12 FIVE-INCH PANCAKES**

1 c. rice flour

¼ c. tapioca flour

¼ c. potato starch

1½ tsp. baking powder

½ tsp. baking soda

½ tsp. salt

¼ tsp. xanthan gum

1½ c. low-fat buttermilk

3 Tbsp. unsalted butter, melted

2 whole eggs

4 Tbsp. granulated sugar

½ tsp. pure vanilla extract

Put the rice flour, tapioca flour, potato starch, baking powder, baking soda, salt, and xanthan gum in a medium bowl and whisk lightly to mix.

In a separate bowl, whisk together the buttermilk, melted butter, eggs, sugar, and vanilla. Add the wet ingredients to the dry ingredients, and mix with a whisk or rubber spatula until the batter is almost smooth; a few small lumps are fine, but try not to overmix.

Spray a nonstick skillet or griddle with some nonstick cooking spray and heat oven medium heat. Pour about ¼ cup of batter onto the skillet, leaving room for more pancakes; repeat until you have a few pancakes in the pan but still enough room to slide in your spatula to flip them. Once the bottom of a pancake is nicely browned and lifts free from the skillet, flip it and cook until the other side is browned as well. Serve right away.

SERVING SIZE: one 5-inch pancake **CALORIES:** 140 **TOTAL FAT:** 4 g **CARBS:** 22 g **DIETARY FIBER:** 0 g **PROTEIN:** 3 g

MULTIGRAIN WAFFLES

These waffles are a great way to start the day—they're full of earthy-nutty flavor and a rustic, appealing texture. At Miraval, I like to use a seven-grain cereal along with oats and wheat bran to make sure they are not only treats but also nutritional powerhouses.

MAKES 4 LARGE WAFFLES OR 6 SMALLER WAFFLES

¼ c. seven-grain cereal (such as Bob's Red Mill or Arrowhead Mills)

¼ c. boiling water

1½ c. all-purpose flour

¾ c. rolled oats

¼ c. brown sugar

2 Tbsp. wheat bran

4 tsp. baking powder

1 tsp. cinnamon

Pinch of salt

2 eggs

1½ c. nonfat milk

¼ c. melted unsalted butter

2 Tbsp. canola oil

2 Tbsp. applesauce

Heat a waffle iron.

In a bowl, combine the seven-grain cereal and boiling water, cover with plastic wrap, and let sit at room temperature for 10 minutes.

Meanwhile, combine the flour, oats, sugar, wheat bran, baking powder, cinnamon, and salt in a medium bowl. In another bowl, whisk together the eggs, milk, butter, oil, and applesauce.

Stir the wet ingredients into the dry, and add the cooked seven-grain cereal. Do not overmix the batter.

Pour the batter into the waffle iron, and cook according to manufacturer's instructions (usually 3 to 5 minutes). Serve immediately.

SERVING SIZE: 1 large waffle **CALORIES:** 370 **TOTAL FAT:** 15 g **CARBS:** 49 g **DIETARY FIBER:** 3 g **PROTEIN:** 10 g

STRAWBERRY PECAN SCONES

A topping of bright, slightly chewy jam and crunchy pecans gives these scones an extra dimension of flavor and texture. Yogurt helps the dough stay moist; I use vanilla yogurt for flavor, but you could use plain and simply add ¼ teaspoon of vanilla extract.

MAKES 16 SCONES

2 c. unbleached all-purpose flour

½ c. sugar

2 tsp. baking powder

½ tsp. baking soda

¼ tsp. kosher salt

3 Tbsp. chilled unsalted butter, cut into small pieces

8 oz. vanilla low-fat yogurt

2 egg whites

¼ c. strawberry or raspberry "no sugar added" spread

2 Tbsp. finely chopped pecans

Heat the oven to 350°F. Lightly spray a baking sheet with nonstick cooking spray. Combine the flour, sugar, baking powder, baking soda, and salt in a large bowl. Cut in the butter with a pastry blender until the mixture resembles coarse meal.

In a small bowl, combine the yogurt and egg whites and whisk to blend. Mix the yogurt mixture into the flour mixture, stirring just until dry ingredients are moistened. (The dough will be sticky.)

Lightly flour the work surface and turn the dough out onto it. With floured hands, knead the dough 4 or 5 times. Transfer to the baking sheet and pat it into an 8-inch circle. Spread the preserves over the round scone, leaving a ½-inch border around the outside (like a pizza) and sprinkle with the pecans. Bake for 15 to 20 minutes or until golden. Cut into 16 wedges.

SERVING SIZE: 1 scone **CALORIES:** 120 **TOTAL FAT:** 3 g **CARBS:** 22 g **DIETARY FIBER:** 1 g **PROTEIN:** 3 g

LEMON-GLAZED BLUEBERRY SCONES

The key to tender scones is being gentle with the dough, which is why I suggest mixing the ingredients with your hands. Work the dough just until it holds together; more vigorous kneading will develop too much gluten in the flour, which would make the texture heavy and tough. **MAKES 16 SCONES**

SCONES

2 c. all-purpose flour

½ c. sugar

1 Tbsp. baking powder

2 oz. unsalted butter, cut into small pieces

½ c. nonfat milk

1 whole egg

1½ tsp. lemon zest

1 c. fresh or frozen blueberries

GLAZE

½ c. powdered sugar

1 Tbsp. lemon juice

MAKE THE SCONES: Heat the oven to 350°F. Sift the flour, sugar, and baking powder into a medium-size bowl. Cut in the butter, using a pastry knife or by pinching with your fingers, until the butter and dry ingredients form small crumbs.

Mix the milk, egg, and zest together and then add to the dry ingredients along with the blueberries. Using your hands, mix until you form a soft dough (being careful not to crush the blueberries in this process).

Line a baking sheet with kitchen parchment and spray with nonstick cooking spray. Shape the dough into a 7-inch round and place on prepared baking sheet. Bake until it is lightly golden brown and springs back slightly when pressed in the center, about 25 minutes. Let cool and cut into 16 wedges.

MAKE THE GLAZE: Whisk the powdered sugar and lemon juice together in a small bowl until smooth. Once the scones have cooled, glaze them by taking a spoon and quickly drizzling the glaze over the scones.

SERVING SIZE: 1 scone   **CALORIES:** 130   **TOTAL FAT:** 3 g   **CARBS:** 24 g   **DIETARY FIBER:** 1 g   **PROTEIN:** 2 g

RAISIN BRAN MUFFINS

These appealing little muffins are full of fiber and contain just the right amount of sweetness. I use prune puree to replace some of the fat that would normally be added, and I make them in mini-muffin tins, which is a perfect size for a satisfying snack.

MAKES 24 MINI MUFFINS (OR 12 REGULAR SIZE)

2 c. wheat bran

2 c. whole-wheat flour

1 Tbsp. baking powder

2 tsp. baking soda

1 tsp. cinnamon

2½ c. low-fat buttermilk

2 whole eggs

¾ c. brown sugar

½ c. honey

¼ c. melted unsalted butter

¼ c. prune puree

¾ c. raisins

To make the prune puree, place canned pitted prunes in a food processor and blend until smooth. (This puree can be stored in the refrigerator for up to seven days.)

Heat the oven to 350°F, and spray mini-muffin tins with nonfat cooking spray.

Put the wheat bran, whole-wheat flour, baking powder, baking soda, and cinnamon in a medium-size bowl and whisk lightly to mix.

In a separate bowl, combine the buttermilk, eggs, brown sugar, honey, melted butter, and prune puree and whisk until smooth. Add the wet ingredients to the dry ingredients, and mix with a whisk or rubber spatula until just combined. Fold in the raisins.

Spoon the batter into mini-muffin tins and bake for 15 minutes until brown and the top springs back when touched. Remove the muffins from the tins, and let them cool to room temperature.

SERVING SIZE: 1 mini muffin **CALORIES:** 120 **TOTAL FAT:** 2.5 g **CARBS:** 24 g **DIETARY FIBER:** 4 g **PROTEIN:** 3 g

CLASSIC BLUEBERRY MUFFINS

A big part of Justin's and my approach at Miraval is showing that you don't have to deprive yourself of good food—you just need to hold things in balance. These muffins are a perfect example! I use low-fat buttermilk and applesauce to keep the fat content lower but include butter and brown sugar for depth of flavor and moist texture. And, of course, blueberries are full of nutrients, so the more of them, the better.

MAKES 24 MINI MUFFINS OR 12 LARGE MUFFINS

1 c. low-fat buttermilk

1 egg

¼ c. melted butter

¼ c. applesauce

1 tsp. vanilla extract

1½ c. lightly packed light or dark brown sugar

2¼ c. unbleached all-purpose flour

1 tsp. baking soda

¼ tsp. kosher salt

2 c. blueberries

Heat the oven to 350°F. Grease a mini-muffin tin with nonstick cooking spray and set aside.

In a small bowl, combine buttermilk, egg, melted butter, applesauce, vanilla, and brown sugar and whisk until almost smooth. (The batter may be slightly clumpy.) In another bowl, combine flour, baking soda, and salt and whisk to blend.

Add the wet ingredients to the dry and mix until just combined. (Do not overmix.) Fold in the blueberries and scoop the batter into the muffin tins using a ¾-ounce scoop or 1½ tablespoons. Bake for 15 minutes or until lightly brown.

SERVING SIZE: 1 mini muffin **CALORIES:** 130 **TOTAL FAT:** 2 g **CARBS:** 25 g **DIETARY FIBER:** 1 g **PROTEIN:** 2 g

GLAZED CINNAMON ROLLS

At Miraval, my pastry team and I make sure that every morning is a delight by serving freshly baked treats such as these old-fashioned rolls. At home, you might want to save these for a special weekend morning, as they do take some time to prepare. The icing gets a delicious tang—and a lower amount of fat—from Neufchâtel cheese, which is a cream cheese-style cheese with about 30 percent less fat than regular cream cheese.

MAKES 24 LARGE ROLLS OR 48 SMALL ROLLS

ROLLS

1 c. warm water

1 c. warm 2 percent milk

1 Tbsp. active dry yeast

2 eggs

¼ c. melted butter

¼ c. canola oil

5 c. all-purpose flour

1 c. whole-wheat flour

1 c. sugar

1 tsp. salt

¼ c. melted unsalted butter (for brushing the dough)

½ c. lightly packed light or dark brown sugar

1 tsp. cinnamon

MAKE THE ROLLS: Grease a 9-inch x 13-inch baking pan with nonstick cooking spray.

In a stand mixer fitted with a dough hook attachment, combine the warm water, milk, and yeast and let sit for 10 minutes or until the yeast has started to bubble gently. Next add the eggs, melted butter, and oil and mix for 1 minute. Add the flours, sugar, and salt. Continue to mix on medium speed until smooth.

Heat the oven to 350°F. Roll the dough out onto a floured surface to form a 24-inch x 7-inch rectangle, about ½ inch thick, and brush with the melted butter. Sprinkle with the brown sugar and cinnamon. Roll lengthwise into a cylinder and cut into 24 pieces.

Transfer the rolls to the prepared pan, placing them ½ inch apart. Let the rolls rise in a warm place for 1 hour, until doubled in size. Bake in the heated oven for 30 minutes until lightly golden brown. When done, remove from the oven and let cool at room temperature before icing.

ICING

2 c. powdered sugar

3 oz. Neufchâtel cheese

1 Tbsp. unsalted butter, melted

1 tsp. pure vanilla extract

MAKE THE ICING: Cream together the powdered sugar, Neufchâtel cheese, melted butter, and vanilla until smooth. Using a palette knife or table knife, spread the icing over the cinnamon rolls.

SERVING SIZE: 1 small roll **CALORIES:** 141 **TOTAL FAT:** 4 g **CARBS:** 24 g **DIETARY FIBER:** 1 g **PROTEIN:** 2 g

CLASSIC VANILLA COFFEECAKE

Most versions of this classic coffeecake are made with high-fat ingredients such as sour cream and butter. I strive to keep that same moist goodness and rich flavor in my Miraval version by using nonfat yogurt in place of the sour cream. Yogurt is fantastic in baking because the acid keeps the crumbs very tender. I like to change the personality of the coffeecake by sprinkling it with various toppings, and I'll sometimes fold in a cup of blueberries or a half cup of chocolate chips or dried fruit. **MAKES 10 PORTIONS**

3 Tbsp. unsalted butter

⅔ c. granulated sugar

1 whole egg

1 egg white

1 tsp. vanilla extract

1 c. nonfat plain yogurt

1⅓ c. all-purpose flour

½ tsp. baking powder (heaping)

½ tsp. baking soda (heaping)

Topping of your choice (½ cup chopped pecans, ½ cup rolled oats, 1 Tbsp. sugar + 1 tsp. cinnamon, or a combination)

Heat the oven to 350°F. Spray an 8 x 8-inch baking pan with nonstick cooking spray.

In a stand mixer fitted with the paddle attachment, cream together the butter and sugar until light and fluffy, about 2 minutes. Add the egg and egg white, and then add the vanilla. Scrape down the sides of the bowl using a rubber spatula, mix for 1 more minute, and then add the yogurt. Mix another few seconds until smooth.

In a separate bowl, sift together the flour, baking powder, and baking soda. Set the mixer to low speed, and slowly incorporate the dry ingredients into the batter, mixing only until the ingredients are blended. Do not overmix or your cake will be tough. Scrape the batter into the prepared pan. Sprinkle the cake with the topping of choice.

Bake until the cake is set and springs back when touched in the middle, about 40 minutes. Let cool at room temperature before cutting into 10 squares.

SERVING SIZE: 1 piece (¹⁄₁₀ of cake) **CALORIES:** 160 **TOTAL FAT:** 3.5 g **CARBS:** 28 g
DIETARY FIBER: 0 g **PROTEIN:** 3 g

CHEDDAR-CHIVE GLUTEN-FREE BREAD

This recipe makes two loaves of bread, but it keeps well—and freezes well, too—so you might as well bake a lot when you're in the baking mood. The bread is wonderful on its own, as a sandwich, or as an accompaniment to a meal. The fresh chives give the bread a wonderful fragrance; experiment with other herbs, too, such as fresh thyme, dill, or rosemary, and try Parmesan cheese instead of cheddar. **MAKES 2 LOAVES (32 TOTAL SERVINGS)**

1½ c. brown rice flour

1 c. sorghum flour

½ c. tapioca flour

½ c. potato starch

1 tsp. xanthan gum

4 tsp. baking powder

1 tsp. baking soda

1 tsp. kosher salt

4 eggs

2 c. low-fat buttermilk

4 Tbsp. honey

¾ c. canola oil

2 c. shredded sharp cheddar

½ c. chopped fresh chives

Heat the oven to 350°F and spray two 5-inch x 8-inch loaf pans with nonstick cooking spray.

In a medium bowl, sift together the rice flour, sorghum flour, tapioca flour, potato starch, xanthan gum, baking powder, baking soda, and salt. Set aside.

In another medium bowl, whisk together the eggs, buttermilk, honey, and oil and then add the cheddar and chives. Add the wet ingredients to the dry ingredients, and mix with a rubber spatula until incorporated.

Pour the batter into the prepared pans and bake for 45 minutes or until golden brown and the top of the loaf springs back when touched. Cool for 30 minutes at room temperature and carefully invert the loaf pans to release the bread. Serve immediately and cut into 16 slices.

If storing for later use, cool further, wrap well, and refrigerate or freeze (slip into a freezer bag). Can be stored in the refrigerator for up to seven days and at room temperature for two days. NOTE: Cut each loaf into 16 slices (making a total of 32 servings).

SERVING SIZE: 1 slice   **CALORIES:** 150   **TOTAL FAT:** 9 g   **CARBS:** 15 g   **DIETARY FIBER:** 1 g   **PROTEIN:** 4 g

ROSEMARY, GARLIC, and HONEY FOCACCIA

I like to add just a touch of sweetness to this flatbread by mixing some honey with the fresh rosemary and garlic. The flavorings are subtle and complex and let the natural nuttiness of the whole-wheat flour shine through. I think this is a great recipe for a bread-baking novice because even though the dough is wet, it's easy to shape by simply pressing into the baking sheet . . . not to mention that it's delicious! **MAKES 16 SERVINGS**

1 c. warm water

2 Tbsp. honey

1 Tbsp. active dry yeast

¼ c. olive oil

1 c. whole-wheat flour, more if needed

1½ c. unbleached all-purpose flour

1½ tsp. salt

1 Tbsp. chopped fresh rosemary

2 tsp. minced fresh garlic

In a large bowl, combine the water and 1 tablespoon of the honey. Sprinkle the yeast over the surface and let rest for 10 minutes. Stir in 3 tablespoons of the olive oil, both flours, and the salt. Stir, adding more flour if necessary to make a soft dough. The dough will be quite wet and slack; you can use a bit more flour to make handling easier, but don't add too much or the focaccia will be heavy.

Knead the dough for 8 minutes by hand or by using a stand mixer with a dough hook attachment for about 5 minutes.

Spray a large bowl with cooking spray and add the dough. Cover and let stand in a warm place for 1½ hours or until about doubled in size.

Heat the oven to 400°F and grease an 8-inch x 8-inch baking sheet (with an edge) with nonstick cooking spray. Combine the remaining 1 tablespoon oil, rosemary, garlic, and the remaining 1 tablespoon honey in a saucepan and heat over low heat for 1 minute; let cool to room temperature.

When the dough is ready, punch it down gently, just to deflate it back to its original size; place it in the center of the prepared baking pan. Stretch dough to fit the pan, working slowly from the center outward, taking care not to tear the dough. Brush with the rosemary-garlic-honey oil.

Bake the focaccia for 15 to 20 minutes, until golden brown and crisp on the surface. Cool at room temperature and then cut into 16 squares.

SERVING SIZE: 1 piece ($\frac{1}{16}$ of recipe)   **CALORIES:** 140   **TOTAL FAT:** 4 g   **CARBS:** 29 g
DIETARY FIBER: 1 g   **PROTEIN:** 1 g

ROASTED POBLANO CORNBREAD

This is one of the Miraval guests' favorite breads, and Justin and I love it, too. I serve it as an accompaniment to dinner, but at home, we'll often just eat it as a snack bread, maybe served with a little cream cheese or a bowl of salsa for dipping! **MAKES 16 SERVINGS**

1 c. unbleached all-purpose flour

½ tsp. baking soda

1 c. cornmeal

¾ tsp. kosher salt

1¼ c. low-fat buttermilk

2 eggs

¼ c. melted butter

½ c. granulated sugar

1 medium roasted poblano chili (cored, skinned, seeds removed, and minced)

1 c. roasted corn, cut off the cob

½ medium red bell pepper, minced

Heat the oven to 350°F. Line an 8-inch x 8-inch baking pan with parchment cut to fit and then spray with nonstick cooking spray.

In a medium bowl, sift together the all-purpose flour and baking soda and then whisk in the cornmeal and salt. In a separate bowl, whisk together the buttermilk, eggs, melted butter, and sugar.

Add the wet ingredients to the dry and mix just until smooth. Fold in the chili, corn, and bell pepper. Pour into the prepared pan and bake for 20 to 25 minutes or until it is lightly brown around the edges and springs back in the center when touched.

SERVING SIZE: 1 piece (1/16 of recipe)   **CALORIES:** 130   **TOTAL FAT:** 4 g   **CARBS:** 21 g   **DIETARY FIBER:** 1 g   **PROTEIN:** 3 g

HEARTY SEVEN-GRAIN BREAD

We love having a loaf of this bread at home. I can reach for it whether I'm making toast, sandwiches, or some French toast for a Sunday morning. I love the mix of grains that I get by using a seven-grain cereal mix, and a generous amount of agave nectar makes the bread nicely moist and very slightly sweet. **MAKES 2 NINE-INCH ROUND LOAVES, 16 SLICES EACH**

¼ c. warm water

1½ Tbsp. active dry yeast

2 tsp. granulated sugar

1 c. seven-grain cereal

1 c. very hot water

¼ c. low-fat buttermilk

⅓ c. agave nectar

4 Tbsp. canola oil

1 Tbsp. unsalted butter, melted

3 whole eggs

4 c. all-purpose flour

1 c. whole-wheat flour

1 Tbsp. kosher salt

In a stand mixer fitted with a dough hook, combine the ¼ cup warm water, the yeast, and the sugar and let sit for 10 minutes until the yeast activates, or "blooms." Meanwhile, combine the hot water and the cereal and let sit at room temperature for 10 minutes until the cereal is fully cooked. Move the cooked cereal to the refrigerator to cool.

Add the buttermilk, agave, oil, melted butter, and eggs to the yeast mixture; mix for a couple minutes on medium speed. Then add in the cereal, both flours, and salt. Mix for 5 minutes, until the dough is smooth and elastic. (If the dough is too sticky, add a couple more tablespoons of flour so that the dough will pull away from the side of the bowl.) Transfer the dough to a greased bowl, cover, and let sit in a warm place for 1½ hours or until doubled in size.

Heat the oven to 375°F and line a baking sheet with kitchen parchment. Roll the dough into 2 round loaves and place on the baking sheet 6 inches apart. Cover with plastic wrap and let dough rise again until almost doubled in size, about 25 minutes. Bake for 35 to 40 minutes until golden brown or until the loaves reach an internal temperature of 165°F. When tapped on the bottom the loaves should sound hollow. Remove from the oven and cool.

SERVING SIZE: 1 slice (32 total servings) **CALORIES:** 130 **TOTAL FAT:** 3 g **CARBS:** 22 g **DIETARY FIBER:** 1 g **PROTEIN:** 4 g

WHOLE-WHEAT HONEY OAT ROLLS

Every baker has a handful of recipes that are their "go-to" favorites, and this is one of mine. These rolls are so versatile—they go with anything, from a big homey Thanksgiving feast to a fancy dinner party, and they're also great for making mini turkey sandwiches. The small amount of honey keeps the sweetness subtle but somehow brings out the nuttiness of the whole-wheat flour. **MAKES 16 ROLLS**

¼ c. warm water

2½ tsp. active dry yeast

3 oz. unsalted butter, melted

2 eggs

1 c. nonfat milk

2 Tbsp. sugar

3 c. all-purpose flour

1½ c. whole-wheat flour

2 tsp. salt

2 Tbsp. honey

2 Tbsp. nonfat milk

½ c. rolled oats

In a stand mixer fitted with a dough hook, combine the warm water and yeast and let sit for 10 minutes until the yeast is activated. Add the melted butter, eggs, milk, and sugar and mix for 1 minute.

Next, add the all-purpose flour, whole-wheat flour, and the salt. Mix for 7 minutes or until smooth and elastic. Transfer dough to a greased medium-size bowl and cover with plastic wrap. Let the dough rise at room temperature for 1½ hours or until doubled in size.

Line a sheet pan with parchment and spray nonstick cooking spray. Divide the dough into 16 portions and roll into balls; arrange the balls on the prepared sheet pan. Cover the rolls with plastic wrap and let them rise again at room temperature for 30 minutes.

Heat the oven to 350°F. In a small bowl, combine the honey and 2 Tbsp. milk and brush the rolls with the mixture. Sprinkle the rolls with oats. Bake in the heated oven for 45 minutes or until golden brown.

SERVING SIZE: 1 roll **CALORIES:** 200 **TOTAL FAT:** 6 g **CARBS:** 33 g **DIETARY FIBER:** 2 g **PROTEIN:** 6 g

PRETZEL BREAD ROLLS

I use a baking soda–water solution to give this bread a nice dark brown color, a characteristic of most pretzels. Using a spray bottle helps to coat the dough well without having to go through the messy, time-consuming process of boiling the dough in the solution prior to baking. The dough has a sweet flavor that is offset by the salty exterior. As the names suggests, I roll the dough into rolls as opposed to a pretzel shape, making this bread very quick and easy to make. **MAKES ABOUT 35 ROLLS**

6 tsp. active dry yeast

2¼ c. warm water

¾ c. plus 1 tsp. granulated sugar

7 c. all-purpose flour

2¼ tsp. kosher salt, plus more for sprinkling

2 Tbsp. canola oil

¼ c. baking soda

2 c. warm water

In a mixer fitted with a dough hook attachment, briefly blend the yeast, warm water, and 1 teaspoon of the sugar. Let rest about 10 minutes so it can "bloom" to activate the yeast.

After yeast has activated, add the flour, remaining ¾ cup sugar, salt, and oil. Mix for 5 minutes or until a smooth, dense dough has formed.

Remove the dough from the mixer and transfer to a greased medium-sized bowl. Let the dough rise in a warm place for 2 hours or until doubled in size.

Line a baking sheet with kitchen parchment and spray it with nonstick cooking spray. Divide the dough into 3 equal pieces and roll each piece into a rope about 2 inches in diameter. Cut each rope into 1½-inch pieces. This should give you roughly 35 rolls.

Place the rolls on the prepared baking sheet about 2 inches apart. Cover with a clean dishcloth and let rise again for 30 minutes.

Heat the oven to 425°F. In another bowl, combine the baking soda and warm water. Transfer the baking soda solution to a spray bottle and spray the rolls generously with the solution. Sprinkle with extra kosher salt if you like. Bake for 15 minutes until the rolls are a rich dark brown all over. Remove from the oven and let cool on the baking sheet.

SERVING SIZE: 1 roll **CALORIES:** 120 **TOTAL FAT:** 1 g **CARBS:** 24 g **DIETARY FIBER:** 1 g **PROTEIN:** 3 g

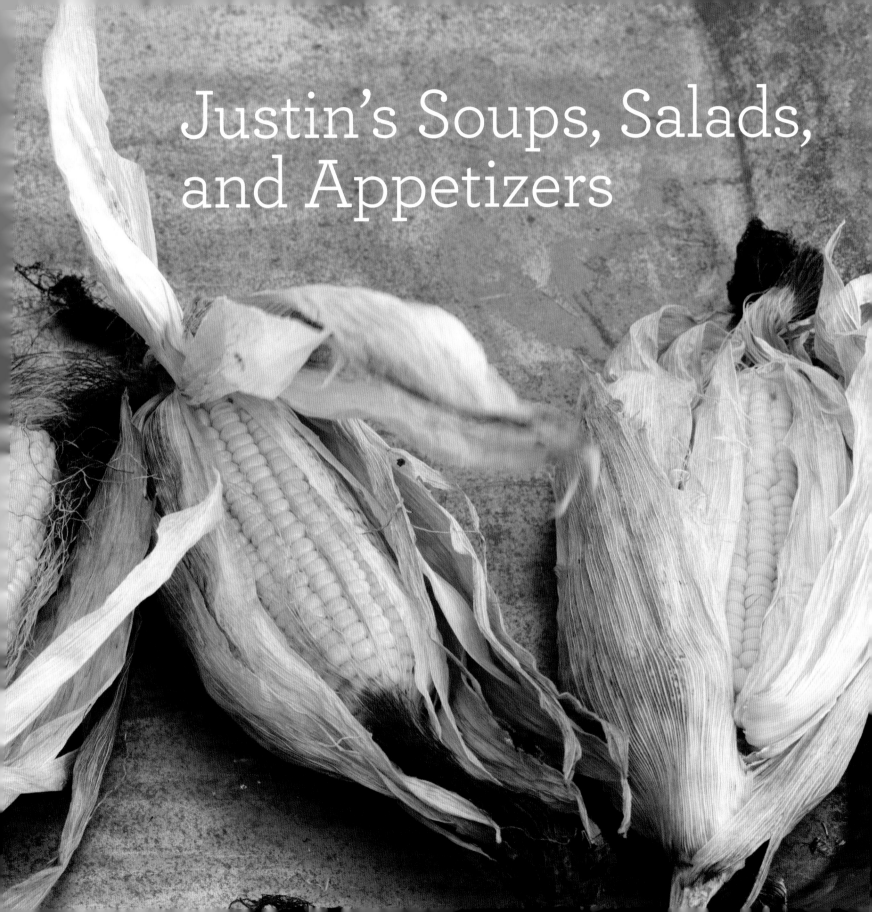

Justin's Soups, Salads, and Appetizers

POTATO LEEK SOUP

Making a pot of this warming soup is an easy way to take home the taste of Miraval. When you puree the finished soup, the potatoes give it a lovely creamy texture without any cream. I like to use Yukon Golds, which are a medium-starch potato with a nice nutty flavor. **SERVES 4**

2 tsp. extra-virgin olive oil

2 lb. Yukon Gold potatoes, peeled and cut into small chunks

2 c. chopped leeks, white part only

2 c. chopped celery

2 tsp. minced fresh garlic

1 tsp. fresh thyme

1 tsp. kosher salt

½ tsp. ground white pepper

7 c. vegetable stock (see page 116)

Heat a large stockpot over high heat. Add olive oil, potatoes, leeks, celery, garlic, and thyme and season with the salt and pepper. Reduce the heat to medium and gently sauté the vegetables, stirring continuously, until the leeks are translucent, about 5 minutes.

Stir in the vegetable stock and bring to a boil. Reduce the heat and simmer for 15 to 20 minutes or until potatoes are soft and falling apart.

Carefully ladle the soup into a blender and puree until smooth. (You may need to do this in batches.) Strain the soup through a fine mesh strainer (or you can skip straining and serve with a more rustic texture, if you like). Taste and adjust seasonings with more salt and pepper if needed.

SERVING SIZE: 4 ounces **CALORIES:** 270 **TOTAL FAT:** 2.5 g **CARBS:** 54 g **DIETARY FIBER:** 6 g **PROTEIN:** 7 g

OYSTER MUSHROOM SOUP

Oyster mushrooms are "wild" mushrooms that are now cultivated and therefore available in many good grocery stores. The pearly gray mushrooms grow in clusters and have a mild, slightly woodsy flavor. You can mix them with other varieties of mushroom if you like, such as maitake, cremini, or shiitake. **SERVES 5**

¼ tsp. extra-virgin olive oil

2 c. chopped onion

1 c. chopped celery

9 c. chopped oyster mushrooms, or a mix of other wild mushrooms

1 Tbsp. finely minced garlic

3 c. peeled and chopped potatoes

8 c. vegetable stock (see page 116)

2 tsp. dried thyme

1 bay leaf

1 tsp. kosher salt

⅛ tsp. freshly ground black pepper

Add the olive oil to a medium stockpot and heat over medium-high heat. Add the onion, celery, mushrooms, and garlic and cook for about 2 minutes to soften the onions. Stir in the potatoes for about 1 minute. Stir in the stock, thyme, bay leaf, salt, and pepper. Bring to a boil, reduce the heat, and then simmer for 20 to 25 minutes until the potatoes are very soft and starting to fall apart.

Remove the bay leaf. Carefully ladle the soup into a blender and puree until smooth. (You may need to do this in batches.) Strain the soup through a fine mesh strainer and return to the pot to reheat. Adjust seasoning with more salt and pepper if needed.

SERVING SIZE: 4 ounces **CALORIES:** 170 **TOTAL FAT:** 1 g **CARBS:** 34 g **DIETARY FIBER:** 5 g **PROTEIN:** 8 g

ROASTED CORN SOUP

Roasting the corn over a gas flame or grill gives it a toasty flavor that, when paired with the chilies, gives this soup a nice Southwestern flavor. Even with the kernels removed, corncobs are loaded with sweet corn flavor, so I simmer one of them with the broth for a richer result. **SERVES 4 TO 5**

4 to 5 ears fresh corn, husks and silks removed

1 Tbsp. Miraval Oil Blend (see page 118)

2 cloves garlic, minced

½ c. chopped carrot

½ c. chopped red or yellow onion

½ c. chopped celery

½ tsp. ground cumin

2 yellow bell peppers, roasted, peeled, and seeded

1 Anaheim chili, cored, seeded, and chopped

4 c. chicken or vegetable stock

1 c. rice milk

Kosher salt to taste

Freshly ground black pepper to taste

Hold the ears of corn over an open flame in the kitchen or on a grill outside until the kernels have a golden brown look to them. (Use the remaining stalk end as a handle, or insert a large fork into the cob.) Once cooled, cut off the kernels and set them aside; you should have about 4 cups. Reserve one of the corncobs.

In a large sauté pan, heat the oil over medium heat and sauté the garlic, carrot, onion, and celery until soft and fragrant and starting to caramelize just a bit, about 5 minutes. Add the corn kernels, cumin, and bell peppers and sauté for another 3 minutes. Add the Anaheim chili, chicken stock or vegetable stock, and the rice milk.

Add the reserved corncob to the soup, lower the heat, and simmer for about 30 minutes, until the vegetables are very soft. Carefully ladle the soup into a blender and puree until smooth. (You may need to do this in batches.) Strain through a fine mesh strainer and season with salt and pepper. Reheat just before serving, if needed.

SERVING SIZE: 4 ounces **CALORIES:** 230 **TOTAL FAT:** 7 g **CARBS:** 36 g **DIETARY FIBER:** 4 g **PROTEIN:** 8 g

CHARRED ROMA TOMATO and BASIL SOUP

Charring the tomatoes, by broiling them until nicely browned, creates a smoky flavor that balances beautifully with their sweetness. This is a great technique to use on other summer vegetables, especially eggplant, peppers, and sweet onions. At the restaurant, I serve this soup with some house-made crackers and caramelized onions, but to keep things simple at home, a sprinkling of fresh basil is all you need. **SERVES 4**

16 roma tomatoes

2 Tbsp. canola oil

1 small white onion, chopped

1 Tbsp. dried basil

3 small cloves garlic, minced

3 c. chicken or vegetable broth

Kosher salt to taste

Pepper to taste

4 tsp. finely sliced basil leaves

Cut the tomatoes in half lengthwise and arrange them on a rimmed baking sheet lined with parchment, cut side down. Heat the broiler and then broil the tomatoes until their skins are nicely charred and the tomatoes are starting to shrivel up. When cool enough to handle, chop roughly; be sure to reserve all the juices.

Heat the oil in a medium saucepan over medium heat. Add the onion, basil, and garlic and sauté until the onions are just translucent, about 3 minutes. Add the tomatoes and their juices, the broth, and season to taste with salt and pepper. Let the mixture simmer for about 30 minutes. Depending on the amount of moisture in the tomatoes you may need to add more liquid.

Carefully ladle the soup into a blender and puree until smooth. (You may need to do this in batches.) Strain the soup through a fine mesh strainer to remove skins and seeds and return to the pan to reheat. Taste and adjust seasoning. To serve, top each serving with the sliced basil.

SERVING SIZE: 4 ounces **CALORIES:** 150 **TOTAL FAT:** 8 g **CARBS:** 18 g **DIETARY FIBER:** 5 g
PROTEIN: 4 g

ROASTED EGGPLANT SOUP

My menus at Miraval are always inspired by the seasons, and this soup is an example of something I'll serve in the height of summer when all these vegetables are at their peak, especially meaty eggplants. Roasting the vegetables first concentrates their flavors and enhances their natural sweetness, which is why this soup is so delicious. **SERVES 4**

1 large eggplant, about 1½ pounds

2 medium tomatoes

2 red bell peppers

1 yellow onion, peeled

1 Tbsp. extra-virgin olive oil

8 garlic cloves

4 c. vegetable stock (see page 116)

2 Tbsp. roughly chopped fresh basil

1 Tbsp. fresh oregano leaves

1 Tbsp. fresh thyme sprigs

Kosher salt to taste

Cayenne pepper to taste

Lemon juice to taste

Heat the oven to 375°F. Cut the eggplant into large chunks, halve the tomatoes and peppers, and quarter the onions. Toss them all with the olive oil and the garlic and then spread the vegetables onto rimmed baking sheets; you'll need more than one.

Roast until the vegetables are very soft, collapsed, and starting to brown around the edges, 35 to 45 minutes, depending on their size.

When cool enough to handle, pull out the core and seeds from the bell peppers and then put all the vegetables into a large stockpot. Add the vegetable stock, basil, oregano, and thyme and season generously with salt and just a pinch of cayenne. Simmer until the soup has reduced by about one-third and is concentrated in flavor. Carefully ladle the soup into a blender and puree until smooth. (You may need to do this in batches.)

Strain the soup through a fine mesh strainer to remove skins and seeds and return to the pan to reheat. Taste, adding a little lemon juice, and adjust seasonings before serving.

SERVING SIZE: 4 ounces   **CALORIES:** 130   **TOTAL FAT:** 6 g   **CARBS:** 16 g   **DIETARY FIBER:** 8 g   **PROTEIN:** 7 g

GREEN SALAD with a CRISPY "VASE" and BLUE CHEESE CRUMBLES

Eggroll wrappers are the caterer's secret weapon, and home cooks can use them, too, to create beautifully presented appetizers. In this salad, I bake the wrappers so they form crisp containers for the fresh salad ingredients. The lavender adds an herbal-floral touch that pairs really nicely with the blue cheese. SERVES 4

4 eggroll wrappers

1 Tbsp. dried lavender (optional)

⅓ c. red wine vinegar

1 clove garlic, minced

1 Tbsp. Dijon mustard

1 tsp. honey

Kosher salt to taste

Freshly ground black pepper to taste

2 Tbsp. olive oil

4 c. mixed salad greens

2 roma tomatoes, cut into quarters

½ c. crumbled blue cheese

MAKE THE CRISPY VASES: Heat the oven to 350°F. Cut the eggroll wrappers in half like a triangle. Take the two bottom ends and bring them together in a circle. Tuck each wrapper into a muffin pan upright and put a handful of uncooked dried beans in the center to hold the wrapper in place and keep its shape. Fold the top back to make a collar, spray with nonstick cooking spray, and sprinkle crushed lavender, if using. Pop the wrappers into the oven until golden brown, 3 to 5 minutes.

MAKE THE DRESSING: Put the vinegar, garlic, mustard, and honey in a small bowl and whisk to blend. Season generously with salt and pepper to taste. Slowly whisk in the oil until the dressing is blended and slightly creamy.

ASSEMBLE THE SALAD: Toss the salad greens with just enough dressing to moisten and flavor them lightly. Place a crispy vase on each plate and fill with the salad mix with some tumbling out. Arrange the tomatoes in front, drizzle on a bit more dressing, and finish with the crumbled blue cheese. Serve right away.

SERVING SIZE: ½ cup CALORIES: 230 TOTAL FAT: 13 g CARBS: 22 g DIETARY FIBER: 1 g PROTEIN: 7 g

ROMAINE and TOASTED PINE NUT SALAD

Cotija is a Mexican cheese that we're very familiar with at Miraval, given our location in the Southwest. It's a cow's milk cheese that's slightly dry and crumbly, quite salty, and with just a touch of tang. It's delicious in salads, but if you can't find cotija, you can substitute Parmesan or feta. **SERVES 4**

2 garlic cloves, minced

1 tsp. Dijon mustard

2 Tbsp. red wine vinegar

¼ tsp. kosher salt

Freshly ground black pepper to taste

⅓ c. extra-virgin olive oil

1 heart romaine lettuce

¼ c. toasted pine nuts

¼ c. grated cotija cheese

Put the minced garlic, mustard, and vinegar in a small bowl and whisk to blend. Add the salt and season to taste with the black pepper. Slowly whisk in the olive oil until the dressing is blended and slightly creamy.

Trim off the root end of the romaine heart and cut it across into 1-inch slices. Put the lettuce into a large mixing bowl. Add the toasted pine nuts, cotija cheese, and the dressing. Toss until well mixed; serve immediately.

SERVING SIZE: ½ cup   **CALORIES:** 250   **TOTAL FAT:** 26 g   **CARBS:** 2 g   **DIETARY FIBER:** 0 g **PROTEIN:** 3 g

BLUE-CORN-CRUSTED CALAMARI SALAD with SPICY VINAIGRETTE

If you haven't yet tried panko-style bread crumbs in your own kitchen, now is the time to do so. I use them a lot at Miraval. These Japanese-style dry bread crumbs are larger than the typical dried crumb, and they create a super-crunchy coating without absorbing too much oil. **SERVES 4**

VINAIGRETTE:

3 Tbsp. rice wine vinegar

2 tsp. sambal oelek or other hot chili sauce

2 tsp. extra-virgin olive oil

¼ tsp. xanthan gum

2 tsp. chopped cilantro

BREAD-CRUMB MIX:

¼ c. panko

¼ c. blue cornmeal

1 Tbsp. finely chopped cilantro

Kosher salt to taste

Freshly ground black pepper to taste

CALAMARI:

¼ lb. calamari, cleaned, tubes cut into ½-inch rings and tentacles cut in half if large

1 tsp. olive oil

1 Tbsp. lemon juice

MAKE THE VINAIGRETTE: Put the vinegar, sambal, and olive oil in a blender and process until creamy and emulsified. Add the xanthan gum and process again for a few seconds. Pour into a container and whisk in the fresh chopped cilantro.

Heat the oven to 400°F. In a large bowl, whisk together the panko, cornmeal, cilantro, and salt and pepper to taste. Put the calamari in another bowl and toss with the oil and lemon to coat evenly.

Add some calamari pieces to the breading, toss to coat thoroughly, and then arrange them evenly on a baking sheet. Repeat with the rest of the calamari.

Bake until the calamari is crisp and golden brown, 6 to 8 minutes.

IF YOU WANT TO MAKE THE TORTILLA CUPS: cut the tortillas into quarters. Spray a large muffin tin with nonstick cooking spray, tuck a tortilla quarter into a muffin pocket, and bake until crisp, about 10 minutes.

(CONTINUED)

4 chipotle-flavored flour tortillas

2 c. mixed salad greens

To serve, toss the greens with some vinaigrette just until lightly moistened. Pile some greens on each plate and top with some calamari; drizzle with a bit more vinaigrette if you like. If serving the tortilla cups, arrange the cup on its side on the plate and then arrange the greens so they're tumbling out of the cup.

SERVING SIZE: ½ cup   **CALORIES:** 190   **TOTAL FAT:** 7 g   **CARBS:** 24 g   **DIETARY FIBER:** 2 g
PROTEIN: 8 g

ARUGULA and MAINE LOBSTER SALAD with VANILLA BEAN VINAIGRETTE

The method I use at Miraval for the asparagus is easy and results in attractive, fresh green curls. Be sure to choose nice, fat asparagus spears so you have enough to peel. If can only find the skinny spears, you can still make a version of this salad that will be delicious. Simply trim away the woody base of the asparagus and cut the spears at an angle into very thin slices. **SERVES 4**

4 raw asparagus spears (Don't use very thin ones.)

4 loosely packed cups arugula greens

⅓ cup Vanilla Bean Vinaigrette (recipe follows)

12 ounces cooked Maine lobster tail, cut into medallions

Using a vegetable peeler, peel the raw asparagus spears into thin, lengthwise ribbons and place in a bowl of ice water until they begin to curl up.

In a large mixing bowl, combine arugula greens and just enough vinaigrette to moisten the greens. Mix well.

Drain the asparagus curls well on paper towels and then place equal amounts of the curls in the centers of four chilled plates. Top with equal amounts of arugula greens. Arrange lobster medallions around the greens, drizzle on a bit more vinaigrette, and enjoy.

SERVING SIZE: ½ cup **CALORIES:** 90 **TOTAL FAT:** 2 g **CARBS:** 2 g **DIETARY FIBER:** 1 g **PROTEIN:** 16 g

VANILLA BEAN VINAIGRETTE

MAKES 1 CUP

¼ tsp. minced garlic

1½ tsp. fresh mixed herbs

¾ c. vanilla-infused rice wine vinegar (see directions)

⅛ tsp. kosher salt

Pinch freshly ground black pepper

½ tsp. vanilla extract

1 whole egg

1 tsp. extra-virgin olive oil

Put the garlic, herbs, vinegar, salt, pepper, and vanilla extract in a blender. Blend for a minute or so and then add the egg and oil and continue to blend until the dressing is very creamy. Keep warm or cold and serve over your favorite greens or fish.

TO MAKE THE VANILLA-INFUSED RICE WINE VINEGAR: bring just under one cup of rice wine vinegar to a boil and then pour into a heat-proof container. Add one whole vanilla bean; cover and let sit for one hour. (The longer it sits, the better the flavor.) Remove the vanilla bean and discard.

SERVING SIZE: 2 tablespoons CALORIES: 15 TOTAL FAT: 1 g CARBS: 0 g DIETARY FIBER: 0 g PROTEIN: 1 g

SCALLOPS with LEMON VINAIGRETTE and FRISÉE

It's important to select your scallops carefully because many that you'll find in a grocery store are what we call "wet," meaning they've been treated with a preservative that plumps them up. Not only will you be paying for the weight of the liquid but the texture of these scallops also isn't good, and they will not develop a nice caramelized surface when you cook them. Ask for "dry-pack" scallops. At Miraval, I slip a nice sliver of black truffle into each scallop, but at home you can just use truffle oil to get that wonderful flavor. **SERVES 4**

4 large dry-pack sea scallops (2 to 3 oz. each)

Kosher salt to taste

Freshly ground black pepper to taste

2 c. washed and dried frisée, torn into bite-size pieces

1 Tbsp. Lemon Vinaigrette (recipe follows)

1½ tsp. truffle oil

Season the scallops with salt and pepper. Heat a heavy skillet, preferably cast iron, over high heat and add the scallops to the pan. Sear until just barely cooked through and nicely browned on the surface, 2 to 3 minutes.

To assemble, toss the frisée thoroughly with the vinaigrette and arrange on plates. Nestle some scallops onto the greens and drizzle truffle oil over the salads. Serve right away.

SERVING SIZE: 1 scallop   **CALORIES:** 110   **TOTAL FAT:** 7 g   **CARBS:** 3 g   **DIETARY FIBER:** 0 g   **PROTEIN:** 9 g

LEMON VINAIGRETTE

MAKES ½ CUP

Finely grated zest and juice of 2 large lemons

1 tsp. Dijon mustard

Kosher salt to taste

Freshly ground black pepper to taste

3 hard-cooked egg yolks

2 Tbsp. extra-virgin olive oil

Put the lemon zest, lemon juice, mustard, and some salt and pepper in a blender or food processor and blend until smooth. Add the egg yolks and process a few more seconds. With the motor running, slowly add the oil.

SERVING SIZE: 1 tablespoon **CALORIES:** 50 **TOTAL FAT:** 5 g **CARBS:** 0 g **DIETARY FIBER:** 0 g **PROTEIN:** 1 g

CRAB WONTONS with SOY-GINGER DIPPING SAUCE

These wontons are a favorite at Miraval, and they're fun to make and serve at home, too. If you can't get crab, you can substitute chopped cooked shrimp or even smoked salmon. The Soy-Ginger Dipping Sauce will last for days, so feel free to make extra and use it to drizzle on steamed vegetables and rice for a quick dinner. **SERVES 8**

¼ c. panko bread crumbs

¾ c. cream cheese

⅓ c. finely diced red pepper

2 Tbsp. green onions, thinly cut on the bias

2 Tbsp. minced shallots

⅛ tsp. salt

Pinch freshly ground black pepper

2 oz. crab meat, picked over to remove any shell

¾ tsp. lemon zest

16 wonton wrappers

Heat the oven to 350°F. Spread the bread crumbs in an even layer on a baking sheet and toast until they're a light golden color, about 8 minutes.

Pulse the cream cheese in a food processor until smooth. Transfer to a large mixing bowl. Stir in the red pepper, green onion, shallots, salt, pepper, bread crumbs, crab, and lemon zest. Mix gently until well blended.

Put the mixture into a large zip-top bag; snip off one of the lower corners.

Arrange the wonton wrappers on a dry, clean surface. Pipe about 2 tablespoons of the crab mixture into the center of each wonton; lightly brush a little water on the edges of the wonton to help seal the wonton. Bring the top right corner and the bottom left corner to a point and pinch; then bring your bottom right corner in and pinch. Repeat the same with the other corner to form a pouch.

To bake, increase the oven temperature to 400°F. Spray a baking sheet with nonstick cooking spray. Arrange the wontons on the baking sheet and spray each one with a very light coat of cooking spray. Bake until golden brown, or about 6 minutes. Serve two pieces for each serving immediately with dipping sauce.

SERVING SIZE: 2 wontons **CALORIES:** 160 **TOTAL FAT:** 8 g **CARBS:** 16 g **DIETARY FIBER:** 1 g **PROTEIN:** 5 g

SOY-GINGER DIPPING SAUCE

MAKES ABOUT 1⅓ CUPS

3 Tbsp. sugar

1⅓ c. rice wine vinegar

2 Tbsp. minced fresh ginger

1½ Tbsp. soy sauce or tamari

½ tsp. xanthan gum

In a medium saucepan, combine the sugar and rice wine vinegar and bring to a simmer. Add the fresh minced ginger. Continue to simmer for 4 minutes. Add the soy sauce or tamari and the xanthan gum, and whisk until well incorporated. Chill until ready to serve.

SERVING SIZE: 1 tablespoon **CALORIES:** 10 **TOTAL FAT:** 0 g **CARBS:** 3 g **DIETARY FIBER:** 0 g **PROTEIN:** 0 g

ROASTED BABY BEET SALAD with HONEY MUSTARD DRESSING

I like to play with the colors and shapes of different varieties of beets, which I have access to at Miraval. If you can only find one type of large beet, you can get a nice look on the plate by slicing some and cutting others into smaller dice. **SERVES 4**

2 medium beets, roasted, and cut into 8 slices each

12 assorted baby beets, roasted (red, yellow, chiogga)

2 c. washed and dried baby greens (including the beet greens, if they're fresh)

½ c. Honey Mustard Dressing (recipe follows)

To roast a beet, trim off the tops and bottoms, wrap in foil, and roast in a 375°F oven for about an hour, or until completely tender when poked with a knife. When cool enough to handle, slip off the skins.

On each plate, arrange four slices of the large beets in the center in an overlapping petal formation.

In a mixing bowl, combine the baby beets and greens and toss with the dressing. Arrange a nice mound on top of the beet slices. Serve right away.

SERVING SIZE: ½ cup   **CALORIES:** 80   **TOTAL FAT:** 1 g   **CARBS:** 18 g   **DIETARY FIBER:** 3 g
PROTEIN: 2 g

HONEY MUSTARD DRESSING

MAKES 1¼ CUPS

2 Tbsp. Dijon mustard

¼ c. whole-grained Dijon mustard

1 Tbsp. minced shallot

¾ tsp. minced fresh garlic

¼ c. honey

3 Tbsp. apple cider vinegar

¼ c. thickened vegetable stock (see page 117)

1½ tsp. extra-virgin olive oil

⅛ tsp. kosher salt

Pinch white pepper

½ tsp. chopped fresh chives

In a mixing bowl, combine the Dijon mustard, whole-grained mustard, shallot, garlic, honey, and vinegar and whisk to blend well. Add the thickened vegetable stock, oil, salt, pepper, and chives. Whisk to incorporate the vegetable stock and oil. The dressing will be thick and creamy.

SERVING SIZE: 2 tablespoons **CALORIES:** 35 **TOTAL FAT:** 0.5 g **CARBS:** 8 g **DIETARY FIBER:** 0 g **PROTEIN:** 0 g

ARUGULA SALAD with PEAR WALNUT DRESSING and MARINATED BABY ARTICHOKES

Arugula, which is also called rocket, is a favorite ingredient of mine. It's full of nutrients, as are all dark leafy greens, and its peppery flavor really "lifts" a dish. In this salad, the arugula plays perfectly with the sweetness in the pear dressing. Mâche is also a wonderful salad green that grows in tiny clusters, which look pretty on the plate. **SERVES 4**

1½ c. mâche (If the clusters are large, tear them into smaller pieces.)

1½ c. arugula

1½ c. torn Belgian endive (Use the red variety, if you can find it.)

⅓ c. Pear Walnut Dressing (recipe follows)

8 Marinated Baby Artichokes (recipe follows)

1 Tbsp. finely chopped walnuts

Toss the mâche, arugula, and endive in bowl. Toss with the dressing. Divide among four salad plates. Cut the artichokes in half and arrange four artichoke halves on each plate. Sprinkle the walnuts around the salad.

SERVING SIZE: ½ cup **CALORIES:** 310 **TOTAL FAT:** 15 g **CARBS:** 31 g **DIETARY FIBER:** 11 g **PROTEIN:** 7 g

MARINATED BABY ARTICHOKES

I make a double batch of these and have some extras in the fridge to add to pizzas, salads, and sandwiches, in addition to the Arugula Salad with Pear Walnut Dressing. You can make tarragon-infused vinegar at home by filling a sterilized glass jar with four to five sprigs of fresh tarragon, filling it with warmed rice wine vinegar, and letting it refrigerate for a few days.

MAKES 20 BABY ARTICHOKES

½ c. white wine

2 tsp. Dijon mustard

¼ c. tarragon-infused rice wine vinegar

½ c. thickened vegetable stock (see page 117)

2 tsp. extra-virgin olive oil

20 steamed and chilled baby artichokes

In a mixing bowl, combine the wine, mustard, vinegar, stock, and oil. Toss the artichokes with the dressing. Marinate for at least 8 hours in the refrigerator before serving.

SERVING SIZE: 2 baby artichokes   **CALORIES:** 180   **TOTAL FAT:** 4 g   **CARBS:** 26 g
DIETARY FIBER: 10 g   **PROTEIN:** 6 g

PEAR WALNUT DRESSING

MAKES ABOUT ¾ CUP

¼ tsp. extra-virgin olive oil

½ c. peeled and chopped pears

2 Tbsp. finely chopped onion

1 Tbsp. pear brandy

3 Tbsp. infused rice wine vinegar

¼ c. thickened vegetable stock (see page 117)

1 tsp. walnut oil

Heat a sauté pan over medium-high heat and add the olive oil to lightly coat the bottom of the pan. Add the pears and onion and cook until the onions have softened, about 2 minutes. Pour the brandy into the pan and deglaze to dissolve the cooked-on juices. Add the rice wine vinegar, vegetable stock, and walnut oil and stir to combine. Pour all the ingredients into the blender and puree.

SERVING SIZE: 2 tablespoons **CALORIES:** 110 **TOTAL FAT:** 10 g **CARBS:** 4 g **DIETARY FIBER:** 1 g **PROTEIN:** 0 g

THAI NOODLE SALAD

This salad is a great one to have in your back pocket because once you know how to make the dressing and cook the noodles, you can garnish it with any kind of cooked meat, poultry, or seafood, or even diced tofu. If you don't have fish sauce in your pantry yet, this salad is a good motivation to get a bottle. The condiment is very pungent on its own, but used with other ingredients, it brings a special salty accent to Asian dishes that's just delicious. **SERVES 4**

DRESSING

⅓ c. rice wine vinegar

3 Tbsp. lime juice

2 Tbsp. achiote paste

2 Tbsp. green onion

2 Tbsp. cilantro

1 Tbsp. diced jalapeño

1 Tbsp. chopped fresh mint

1 tsp. fish sauce

1 8.8-oz. box rice noodles

1 c. chopped cooked chicken

1 c. chopped cooked shrimp chopped

4 large leaves butter lettuce

MAKE THE DRESSING: Put the vinegar, lime juice, achiote paste, green onion, cilantro, jalapeño, mint, and fish sauce in a blender or food processor and process until smooth.

Soak and cook the noodles according to the package instructions, and then drain well.

Toss the noodles, chicken, and shrimp together with the dressing. Chill the salad for at least one hour to let the flavors marry. To serve, place a lettuce leaf on each plate and arrange some noodle salad on top. Alternatively, chop the butter lettuce and mix with the noodles and serve on a platter family style.

SERVING SIZE: ½ cup   **CALORIES:** 330   **TOTAL FAT:** 2 g   **CARBS:** 52 g   **DIETARY FIBER:** 2 g **PROTEIN:** 24 g

BASIL-LACED ROCKET SALAD with RASPBERRY VINAIGRETTE and HERBED GOAT CHEESE

This salad is a great addition to any summertime lunch or dinner. It's full of fresh flavors that are sure to please your palate. **MAKES ABOUT 6 SERVINGS**

6 c. arugula

2 c. basil, chopped

1 c. Raspberry Vinaigrette

12 toasted pita chips

1 c. Herbed Goat Cheese

RASPBERRY VINAIGRETTE

2 c. rice wine vinegar

2 oz. thickened vegetable stock (see page 117)

2 Tbsp. honey

Pinch salt

½ c. cold-pressed extra-virgin olive oil

4 oz. fresh raspberries

HERBED GOAT CHEESE

1 c. goat cheese

1 tsp. oregano, chopped

1 tsp. thyme, chopped

1 tsp. parsley, chopped

Garlic powder to taste

Salt to taste

Pepper to taste

Cut pita bread into points. Toast in the oven at 350°F until crisp. Chop basil and mix in with arugula. For the vinaigrette, whisk all ingredients together, smashing the fresh raspberries in last. Pour over salad. Roll the goat cheese into little balls and place on salad along with the toasted pita points.

To reduce the amount of calories and fat in this recipe, simply omit a portion of the goat cheese.

SERVING SIZE: ½ cup **CALORIES:** 162 **TOTAL FAT:** 8 g **CARBS:** 14 g **DIETARY FIBER:** 0.83 g **PROTEIN:** 7 g

EGGPLANT BASIL ROLL-UPS with TWO CHEESES and ROASTED TOMATO TRUFFLE SAUCE

At Miraval, I like to serve these Mediterranean-inspired roll-ups as a first course, but you can also make a main dish out of them, especially if you top them with tomato sauce. You need to cut the eggplant into thin, even slices, so if you have a mandoline slicer, now is the time to use it! **MAKES 4 SERVINGS**

1 eggplant, sliced ¼-inch thick

Olive oil

2 medium tomatoes, sliced ⅛-inch thick

12 basil leaves, washed

Freshly ground black pepper

4 Tbsp. grated mozzarella cheese

1 Tbsp. crumbled feta cheese

1 tsp. minced chilies de arbol or dried red chili flakes

Roasted Tomato Truffle Sauce, optional (recipe follows)

Place the eggplant slices in a lightly oiled sauté pan over medium low heat. Cook lightly in order to make the slices moist and pliable.

Lay the eggplant slices flat on the work surface and lay a tomato slice at the bottom of each slice. Place a basil leaf on top of the tomato. Grind some fresh pepper over the basil and tomato and sprinkle a teaspoon of both cheeses and a pinch of the chili on top of the basil leaf. Roll up the eggplant lengthwise to make a nice cylindrical packet. Place each packet seam-side down in the sauté pan. Repeat until all the eggplant is rolled up.

Heat the sauté pan to medium and cook, slightly searing the roll-ups. Turn to brown all sides. Arrange three rolls on each plate and serve warm on their own or with Roasted Tomato Truffle Sauce.

SERVING SIZE: 3 rolls **CALORIES:** 105 **TOTAL FAT:** 6 g **CARBS:** 11 g **DIETARY FIBER:** 4 g **PROTEIN:** 4 g

ROASTED TOMATO TRUFFLE SAUCE

Roasting tomatoes and onions, instead of cooking them on the stovetop, is a super-easy way to make a tomato sauce, and the method develops rich, sweet flavors in the vegetables, too, which gives the sauce a lot of character. You can skip the truffle oil—although I wouldn't, it's delicious—but in any case, only add it to the sauce at the last minute in order to preserve the fragrance.

MAKES 8 SERVINGS

1 tsp. olive oil

½ onion, chopped

6 cloves fresh garlic, chopped

4 large tomatoes, chopped

2 Tbsp. fresh basil, chopped

Kosher salt to taste

Freshly ground black pepper to taste

½ tsp. truffle oil

Heat the oven 350°F and line a rimmed baking sheet with parchment.

Toss the olive oil, onion, garlic, and tomatoes in a bowl. Spread out on the sheet pan in an even layer and bake, turning occasionally, until soft and slightly browned, 20 to 25 minutes. Remove from the oven and cool slightly.

Place all the roasted vegetables and the basil in the blender and blend until slightly chunky, about 5 seconds. Season to taste with salt and pepper. The sauce will keep like this up to four days in the refrigerator.

Just before serving, pour the sauce into a sauté pan and reheat over medium. Remove from stove and add the truffle oil. Serve warm.

SERVING SIZE: 2 tablespoons **CALORIES:** 15 **TOTAL FAT:** 1 g **CARBS:** 2 g **DIETARY FIBER:** 0 g **PROTEIN:** 0 g

RED PEPPER TOFU DIP

The texture of silken tofu is a great substitute for the dairy ingredients that you might typically find in a dip. When pureed, roasted red peppers also become silky and "dippable." If you don't have time to roast fresh peppers, it's fine to use roasted peppers from a jar. Just be sure to drain off any liquid. **MAKES 4 CUPS**

6 red bell peppers, roasted, peeled, seeded, chopped

1 clove garlic, minced

1 tsp. mixed fresh herbs (thyme, oregano, and parsley makes a nice mix)

1 lb. silken tofu

Juice of 2 lemons

Kosher salt to taste

Freshly ground black pepper to taste

Put the roasted peppers, garlic, herbs, and tofu in a food processor and process until smooth. Season with most of the lemon, some salt, and pepper. Taste and adjust with more lemon, salt, or pepper as needed.

Serve with fresh vegetables or flatbread.

SERVING SIZE: ½ cup   **CALORIES:** 40   **TOTAL FAT:** 0.5 g   **CARBS:** 4 g   **DIETARY FIBER:** 1 g   **PROTEIN:** 4 g

TRUFFLED BLACK OLIVE BRUSCHETTA

Miraval guests often ask me for ideas about appetizers they can make when they entertain at home, and I like to suggest bruschetta. It's easy to mix up a topping ahead of time and then simply toast your bread right before guests arrive, assemble the bruschetta, and you're done. My version at Miraval is quite a bit more elaborate, but I've created this simpler version that still brings together all the same great flavors. **MAKES 12 BRUSCHETTE**

1 Tbsp. minced shallot

¼ c. seeded and diced tomato

¼ c. diced good quality pitted black olive, such as kalamata

1 tsp. chopped Italian parsley

1 tsp. thinly sliced fresh basil

½ tsp. chopped garlic

1 Tbsp. balsamic vinegar

2 tsp. truffle oil

¼ c. finely diced buffalo mozzarella or other fresh mozzarella

12 quarter-inch slices whole-wheat artisan baguette, cut at an angle

Olive oil

Put all the ingredients—except the bread and olive oil—in a small bowl, mix gently, cover tightly, and refrigerate at least an hour to let the flavors marry.

Heat the oven to 400°F. Spray the bread with a thin mist of olive oil and bake in the hot oven until crisp, 4 to 5 minutes.

To serve, drain off any liquid that may have accumulated in the topping bowl and then pile about 1 tablespoon of the topping onto each piece of toast. Serve right away.

SERVING SIZE: 1 bruschetta   **CALORIES:** 80   **TOTAL FAT:** 2 g   **CARBS:** 12 g   **DIETARY FIBER:** 1 g   **PROTEIN:** 3 g

Justin's Main Dishes

STEAK with FRESH HERB and SPICE MARINADE

This marinade, which might also be called a "wet rub," is dynamite on beef. Here, I'm seasoning a flat-iron steak, but it's excellent on a tenderloin or standing rib roast, too. You'll have some leftover marinade, which will keep just fine in the refrigerator for up to two weeks. I like to serve the steak with a classic Parmesan risotto as an accompaniment, and it's also great on greens as a main-dish salad. **SERVES 4**

1 c. extra-virgin olive oil

¼ c. fresh thyme

¼ c. fresh oregano

2 Tbsp. fresh chopped basil

2 Tbsp. minced fresh garlic

1 Tbsp. paprika

2 tsp. kosher salt

1 tsp. freshly ground black pepper

1½ lb. flat-iron steak

In a mixing bowl, stir together the oil, thyme, oregano, basil, garlic, paprika, salt, and pepper. Put the mixture in a jar or airtight container and store in the refrigerator until ready to use.

To prepare the steak, rub both sides of the steak with about 2 tablespoons of the mixture and let sit at room temperature for 30 minutes. Heat a grill or grill pan to medium-high, and grill about 4 minutes per side for medium-rare.

Let the steak rest on a plate or platter for 3 or 4 minutes and then slice on an angle. Serve right away or chill and use for steak salad.

CALORIES: 130   **TOTAL FAT:** 14 g   **CARBS:** 0 g   **DIETARY FIBER:** 0 g   **PROTEIN:** 0 g

SEAR-ROASTED PORK TENDERLOIN with CHIPOTLE SAUCE

Pork tenderloin is a great cut of meat. Each one averages about a pound in weight, perfect for four portions or for serving two people with some leftovers. The meat is lean and extremely tender and adapts to all sorts of flavors. In this dish, which is a simplified version of an entrée I serve at Miraval, the mild pork gets paired with a smoky-sweet chipotle sauce. Serve the pork with a simple side, such as quinoa or herbed rice. **SERVES 4**

Olive oil cooking spray

1 one-pound pork tenderloin

⅛ tsp. kosher salt

⅛ tsp. freshly ground black pepper

1 Tbsp. chopped fresh mix of thyme, flat Italian parsley, and oregano

½ c. Chipotle Sauce (recipe follows)

Heat the oven to 400°F. Heat a medium, ovenproof sauté pan over medium-high heat and lightly coat with olive oil cooking spray. Season all sides of the pork tenderloin with salt, pepper, and fresh herbs. Add the pork to the pan and sear on one side for 1 to 2 minutes. Turn and continue searing until browned all over.

Place the pan in the hot oven and finish cooking, another 3 to 5 minutes. Aim for pork that's light pink in the center. Let the pork rest for another 3 to 4 minutes and then cut into slices.

Arrange the pork slices on each plate and drizzle with 2 tablespoons of warm Chipotle Sauce.

CALORIES: 170   **TOTAL FAT:** 4 g   **CARBS:** 9 g   **DIETARY FIBER:** 0 g   **PROTEIN:** 24 g

CHIPOTLE SAUCE

MAKES 1⅓ CUPS

¼ tsp. extra-virgin olive oil

½ c. finely chopped onion

¼ c. finely chopped apricots

1½ tsp. minced fresh garlic

1½ tsp. minced fresh ginger

¾ c. ketchup

⅓ c. apple cider vinegar

2 Tbsp. soy sauce

½ c. lightly packed dark or light brown sugar

1 Tbsp. dry mustard

¼ c. chili sauce

2 canned chipotle peppers, finely chopped

¼ c. orange juice

6 oz. lager-style beer, such as Budweiser or beer of your preference

Heat the olive oil in medium saucepan. Add the onion, apricots, garlic, and ginger. Sauté for about 2 minutes. Add the ketchup, vinegar, soy sauce, brown sugar, mustard, chili sauce, chipotles, orange juice, and beer.

Bring the sauce to a boil, reduce the heat to a simmer, and simmer for about 30 minutes to blend the flavors and thicken the sauce.

SERVING SIZE: 2 tablespoons   CALORIES: 40   TOTAL FAT: 0 g   CARBS: 9 g   DIETARY FIBER: 0 g   PROTEIN: 1 g

RACK of LAMB with DIJON, WHITE BEAN, ARUGULA, and SUN-DRIED TOMATO SALAD

If you've never cooked rack of lamb before, don't be nervous—it's one of the easiest cuts of meat to manage. The rack is simply seven or eight rib chops that are not yet cut apart. When you roast the whole rack, and then cut it into chops, the meat stays juicy and tender. Some of my Miraval dishes are a bit tricky to pull off at home, but this one isn't, and it's terrific for dinner parties. You can make the bean salad ahead of time and then, right before you sit down for your first course, cook the lamb and tent it with foil to rest and stay warm. The meat will be perfect when you're ready to slice and serve the main course. **SERVES 6**

3 c. cooked and drained white beans, such as cannellini or Great Northern (Canned is fine.)

1 c. sun-dried tomatoes, cut into fine strips

¼ c. Honey Mustard Dressing (see page 61)

2 lamb racks, bones cleaned and Frenched (Aim for 2 or 3 chops per person.)

Kosher salt to taste

Freshly ground black pepper to taste

1 Tbsp. chopped fresh thyme, rosemary, or a mix

3 c. arugula

½ c. freshly grated Parmesan

MAKE THE BEAN SALAD: Toss the beans, sun-dried tomatoes, and dressing together. Set aside for at least 20 minutes for the flavors to blend or until ready to serve.

COOK THE LAMB: Heat the oven to 400°F and heat a grill or sauté pan to high. Season both sides of the lamb generously with salt, pepper, and the herbs. Grill or sauté the lamb racks until nicely seared on each side, about 4 minutes per side.

Transfer to a small roasting pan and place in the hot oven. Roast another 4 to 6 minutes for a nice medium rare, about 125°F on an instant-read thermometer. Let the lamb rest for a few minutes.

TO SERVE: Cut the racks into individual chops. Arrange a bed of arugula on each plate, top with some bean salad and Parmesan, and arrange the chops on each plate. Serve right away.

CALORIES: 420   **TOTAL FAT:** 14 g   **CARBS:** 29 g   **DIETARY FIBER:** 6 g   **PROTEIN:** 45 g

VEAL with CARAMELIZED PEARS and SAGE

I like serving fruit with meat, and the flavor of mild, sweet veal goes really well with pears. The trick is to balance the sweetness of the fruit, however, so here I keep things savory by adding some shallot and chopped fresh sage. If you can't find veal, you could make this dish with turkey scaloppini or with medallions of pork tenderloin that you pound to make them thin. **SERVES 4**

2 whole pears, ripe but still firm

1 tsp. sugar

Kosher salt to taste

Freshly ground black pepper taste

1 tsp. olive oil

1 shallot or ¼ onion, finely sliced

2 large sage leaves, finely chopped

½ c. homemade or low-sodium chicken broth

1 lb. veal scallopini

1 Tbsp. all-purpose flour

1 tsp. olive oil

MAKE THE PEARS: Cut the pears in half lengthwise and cut out the core and stem fibers. (You don't need to peel the pears unless the skin is very tough.) Cut again into quarters. Season the pears with the sugar, salt, and pepper to taste.

Heat a large sauté pan over medium-high heat, add the olive oil, and arrange the pears, cut side down. Distribute the shallot slices around the pears and sprinkle the sage over everything. Reduce the heat to medium and cook until the pears are golden brown on the first side and the shallots are beginning to soften, 5 to 8 minutes. Carefully flip the pears and continue cooking until they are very soft and caramelized, stirring the shallots occasionally so they cook evenly. Keep warm in the pan until time to serve the veal.

When it's time to serve, transfer the warm pears to a plate and heat the pan over medium-high. Add the chicken broth and stir to dissolve the cooking juices in the pan. Boil until the juices have reduced to about 2 tablespoons. Remove the pan from the heat.

To cook the veal, heat a large skillet over medium-high and add the olive oil. Dust the scaloppini with the flour, tapping to remove excess, and then add to the hot skillet; try not to overlap the veal pieces. Sauté the veal until lightly browned and just barely cooked through, about 2 minutes per side, more if the pieces are thick.

To serve, arrange one piece of veal on each plate, top with a pear half and some shallots, and drizzle with the deglazed pan juices. Serve right away.

CALORIES: 190   TOTAL FAT: 6 g   CARBS: 8 g   DIETARY FIBER: 1 g   PROTEIN: 24 g

VENISON CHILI

I make this chili with venison when I cook it at Miraval, but you can use beef chuck as well. Don't grind the meat, however; the cubes will give you a really nice texture. You'll simmer the chili for a long time, which will marry the ingredients and make the meat fork-tender. A little bit of bacon and some canned chipotles in adobo give the dish a hint of smokiness that is balanced by a touch of honey and molasses and some nerve from the porter and red wine. **SERVES 6**

¼ lb. applewood smoked bacon

1 lb. medium-diced venison meat or beef-chuck stew meat

2 medium yellow onions, diced

1 red onion, diced

2 jalapeños, seeded and diced

1 c. diced red bell pepper

3 garlic cloves, chopped

¼ c. balsamic vinegar

2 oz. canned chipotle peppers, minced

4 Tbsp. chili powder

1 Tbsp. paprika

1 Tbsp. ground cumin

In a large pot over medium heat, sauté the bacon until crispy. Remove from the pot and set aside. Pour off the excess grease, increase the heat to medium-high, and add the venison. Sauté until the meat is just barely cooked. Remove from the pot and set aside.

To the same pot, add the onions, jalapeños, red pepper, and garlic and sauté over medium-high for about 3 minutes. Add the balsamic vinegar, chipotle, chili powder, paprika, and cumin; stir well. Cook for 3 more minutes. Add back the venison and bacon, stir for 2 minutes, and then add the honey, molasses, porter, red wine, both types of tomato, and beans. Season generously with salt and pepper.

1 Tbsp. honey

1 Tbsp. molasses

1 twelve-ounce bottle of porter, such as Black Butte from Deschutes Brewery

½ c. red wine

1 c. diced fresh tomatoes

¼ c. diced sun-dried tomatoes

2 c. cooked black beans

1 Tbsp. kosher salt

1 Tbsp. ground black pepper

2 Tbsp. chopped cilantro

Adjust the heat to a simmer and cook for another 60 minutes or so. When the chili is thick and the meat is completely tender, add the chopped cilantro, taste for seasoning, and serve.

SERVING SIZE: 1 cup   **CALORIES:** 290   **TOTAL FAT:** 10 g   **CARBS:** 17 g   **DIETARY FIBER:** 2 g   **PROTEIN:** 26 g

SPICE-RUBBED CHICKEN BREASTS with FRESH FRUIT SALSA

This is a simple recipe that has the spirit of Miraval cuisine—fresh, healthful, and delicious—but it's quick to prepare at home. You can improvise with your fruit as you make the salsa, using other berries or mango instead of papaya. You could even toss in some diced jicama for crunch. Take care not to overcook the chicken breasts, however. Boneless breasts are quick to cook and low in fat, but they also can become dry if you don't watch out. **SERVES 6**

FRESH FRUIT SALSA

1 c. diced strawberries

1½ c. diced pineapple

1 c. diced papaya

¼ c. diced kiwifruit (about 1) (optional)

1 tsp. finely shredded fresh mint

1 tsp. finely chopped fresh cilantro

½ c. fresh squeezed orange juice

1 Tbsp. finely chopped green onion

½ tsp. finely chopped jalapeño

CHICKEN

6 boneless, skinless chicken breasts (about 6 ounces each)

1 Tbsp. smoked paprika

1 tsp. ground cumin

1 tsp. kosher salt

Pinch cayenne pepper

MAKE THE SALSA: Combine all the ingredients in a large bowl and mix well. Cover and refrigerate for about 1 hour before serving.

PREPARE THE CHICKEN: Heat a grill or a grill-pan to medium. With a meat pounder or heavy rolling pin, pound the chicken breasts so they're an even thickness.

Stir together the smoked paprika, cumin, salt, and cayenne. Spray both sides of the chicken with nonstick cooking spray and then season both sides with the spices, patting so the spices stick.

Grill the chicken over medium, turning once, just until it's no longer pink in the center, about 3 minutes per side depending on the size and thickness of the chicken. Let the chicken breasts rest for a couple of minutes and then cut into slices at an angle. Arrange the sliced chicken on each plate and mound the salsa next to it, so that some of the salsa covers the chicken. Serve right away.

CALORIES: 240   **TOTAL FAT:** 4.5 g   **CARBS:** 13 g   **DIETARY FIBER:** 2 g   **PROTEIN:** 36 g

DUCK and ASIAN GREENS STIR-FRY

Stir-fry dishes are wonderful opportunities to incorporate lots of healthful vegetables into your meal. Here I like to use bok choy and broccoli, both nutritional powerhouses, with some slices of woodsy, earthy shiitake mushrooms. But you should feel free to use the vegetables that you have on hand—regular cabbage would be good in this, as would some sliced carrots or snow peas. You can also use cooked chicken instead of duck. **SERVES 4**

SAUCE

2 Tbsp. garlic chili paste

2 Tbsp. water

1 Tbsp. rice wine vinegar

2 tsp. tamari or soy sauce

1 tsp. cornstarch

STIR-FRY

2 tsp. vegetable oil (peanut oil works well)

2 tsp. chopped garlic

2 Tbsp. chopped ginger

3 c. broccoli florets

3 c. sliced bok choy

1 c. sliced fresh shiitake mushrooms

2 c. chopped or shredded cooked duck or chicken

Cooked brown rice, warm (optional)

MAKE THE SAUCE: Put the chili paste, water, vinegar, tamari, and cornstarch in a small bowl and stir to blend well. Set aside.

MAKE THE STIR-FRY: Heat the oil over medium-high in a large sauté pan or a wok. Add the chopped garlic and sauté for 30 seconds, stirring quickly so the garlic doesn't burn. Add the chopped ginger, broccoli florets, and sliced bok choy and sauté for 2 minutes. Add the shiitakes and sauté for another minute.

Add the cooked duck or chicken and toss for a few seconds to heat through. (Don't cook too much or the poultry will dry out.) Add the sauce to the pan and heat until it is slightly thickened and all ingredients are hot and nicely coated in sauce. Serve right away alone or with brown rice.

CALORIES: 190   **TOTAL FAT:** 4.5 g   **CARBS:** 15 g   **DIETARY FIBER:** 3 g   **PROTEIN:** 23 g

BBQ CHICKEN FLATBREAD

Having a batch of homemade dough in the freezer means that you can whip up a Miraval-style flatbread any time. Just divide the dough into 12 portions, press them into flat rounds, and wrap each one separately. Pull out as many portions as you want a few hours ahead of time, and let them thaw and proof on the counter. At the restaurant, we frequently serve these flatbreads as first courses, but combined with a green salad, they can become dinner. **SERVES 1**

1 portion basic flatbread dough (¹⁄₁₂ of the recipe; see page 130)

¼ c. Prickly Pear BBQ Sauce (recipe follows)

¼ c. diced grilled chicken

3 oz. diced roasted red bell peppers

3 oz. diced roasted poblano pepper

¼ c. caramelized red onions (see page 125)

1 Tbsp. crumbled cotija cheese

1 tsp. chopped fresh cilantro

Heat the oven to 400°F. Place the flatbread dough on a lightly floured work surface and roll or press it to a ¼-inch round. Transfer it to a baking sheet.

Spread the BBQ sauce evenly over the surface of the dough and distribute the chicken, roasted peppers, poblanos, and caramelized onions on top. Sprinkle the cotija cheese over the flatbread. Bake for 10 minutes or until the cheese is melted and the dough is lightly browned and crisp.

Transfer to a cutting board, cut in wedges, sprinkle with the cilantro, and serve immediately.

CALORIES: 420   **TOTAL FAT:** 11 g   **CARBS:** 54 g   **DIETARY FIBER:** 5 g   **PROTEIN:** 26 g

PRICKLY PEAR BBQ SAUCE

MAKES 1 CUP

½ c. ketchup

½ c. prickly pear syrup

¼ c. apple cider vinegar

1 Tbsp. honey

1 Tbsp. molasses

¼ c. Cajun blackening spice (McCormick's has a good one.)

Put all the ingredients in a small saucepan, bring to a simmer over medium heat, and simmer until the sauce has reduced by half, about 15 minutes. The sauce will keep about 3 weeks in the refrigerator.

SERVING SIZE: 2 tablespoons   **CALORIES:** 60   **TOTAL FAT:** 0 g   **CARBS:** 14 g   **DIETARY FIBER:** 1 g   **PROTEIN:** 0 g

MARGHERITA PIZZA with BASIL PESTO

Nothing beats the classic combination of tomato, mozzarella, and basil. I like to use buffalo mozzarella, which has more tang to it than cow's milk does, but if you can only find cow's milk cheese, that's perfectly fine. By pureeing the cheese, I can get thin, even coverage on the pizza, delivering lots of flavor but less fat. **SERVES 1**

2 oz. fresh buffalo mozzarella (about ¼ of a large ball)

1 portion basic flatbread dough (¹⁄₁₂ of the recipe; see page 130)

1 large roma tomato, cut into 4 thin slices

1 Tbsp. Basil Pesto (recipe follows)

Heat the oven to 400°F. Put the mozzarella in a food processor and blend until smooth.

Place the flatbread dough on a lightly floured work surface and roll or press it to a ¼-inch round. Transfer it to a baking sheet.

Spread the blended smooth mozzarella evenly across the dough, and arrange the sliced tomatoes around the dough. Bake for 10 minutes or until the cheese is melted and the dough is lightly browned and crisp.

Transfer to a cutting board, cut in wedges, drizzle with the pesto, and serve immediately.

CALORIES: 400   **TOTAL FAT:** 17 g   **CARBS:** 40 g   **DIETARY FIBER:** 4 g   **PROTEIN:** 21 g

BASIL PESTO

MAKES ½ CUP

½ c. toasted pine nuts

¼ tsp. kosher salt

2 cloves garlic

10 basil leaves

2 Tbsp. grated Parmesan cheese

¼ c. extra-virgin olive oil

¼ c. water

Place all the ingredients into a blender or food processor blend for 15 to 30 seconds. Pour into a container. Use as needed. The pesto will keep in the refrigerator up to 1 week.

SERVING SIZE: 2 tablespoons   **CALORIES:** 60   **TOTAL FAT:** 7 g   **CARBS:** 1 g
DIETARY FIBER: 0 g   **PROTEIN:** 1 g

MUSHROOM AND RED BELL PEPPER PIZZA

The earthy flavors of this pizza really pop when you drizzle on the balsamic just before serving. Balsamic reduction is one of my "secret weapons." It's so easy to make and will last in your refrigerator for months. A few drops of the sweet, tangy sauce can benefit all kind of dishes, from vegetables to grilled meats. **SERVES 1**

1 portion basic flatbread dough (¹⁄₁₂ of the recipe; see page 130)

¼ cup marinara sauce (see page 120)

2 Tbsp. diced red bell peppers

2 shiitake mushroom caps, sliced thinly

2 Tbsp. grated provolone cheese

2 Tbsp. balsamic reduction (see page 119)

Heat the oven to 400°F.

Place the flatbread dough on a lightly floured work surface and roll or press it to a ¼-inch round. Transfer it to a baking sheet.

Spread the marinara sauce evenly on the pizza. Layer on the bell peppers, mushrooms, and provolone. Bake for 10 minutes or until the cheese is melted and the dough is lightly browned and crisp.

Transfer to a cutting board, cut in wedges, drizzle with the balsamic reduction, and serve immediately.

CALORIES: 340 **TOTAL FAT:** 8 g **CARBS:** 53 g **DIETARY FIBER:** 6 g **PROTEIN:** 14 g

PAELLA

There are as many versions of Spanish paella as there are cooks. Our Miraval paella gets authentic Spanish flavor from both the chorizo (a cured Spanish sausage) and a pinch of smoked paprika as a final touch. Smoked paprika, which is also called pimentón de la Vera, is available in many grocery stores now, as well as at specialty shops. It comes in both sweet (dulce) and hot (picante) styles. I like using the hot one here. **SERVES 4**

2 c. cooked saffron rice (see page 124)

1½ tsp. extra-virgin olive oil

2 shallots, thinly sliced

¼ tsp. chopped garlic

12 trimmed haricot verts or green beans, halved lengthwise

1 Tbsp. diced red bell pepper

¼ c. sliced Spanish chorizo

½ c. dry white wine

8 oz. skinless boneless chicken breast, simmered in lightly salted water until cooked and shredded with a fork

8 jumbo shrimp 13/15, peeled and deveined (remove tail for easier eating)

12 grape or cherry tomatoes, halved

½ c. chicken stock (see page 121)

Kosher salt to taste

Freshly ground black pepper to taste

2 scallions, white and light green parts only, chopped

1 jalapeño, cored and sliced very thin

¼ tsp. hot (picante) smoked paprika

Have your saffron rice cooked and cooled on the side for when it's time to pull the dish together.

Heat the oven to 400°F. Heat a large, deep skillet over high heat. Add the oil, shallots, and garlic and sauté for about 2 minutes, stirring rapidly so the garlic doesn't burn. Add the haricot verts, red bell peppers, and chorizo and sauté for another minute.

Add the white wine and cook until the liquid has reduced to just a few spoonfuls. Add the shredded chicken, shrimp, tomatoes, chicken stock, and a generous pinch of salt and pepper. Simmer for 1 minute.

Add the saffron rice, give it a good stir, and then cover the skillet with tinfoil. Place the skillet in the hot oven and cook to heat through and marry the flavors, 8 or 9 minutes. Remove from the oven, uncover, and stir in the chopped scallion. Divide the paella evenly into four bowls, top with one or two thin slices of jalapeño, and finish with a pinch of hot smoked paprika.

CALORIES: 390   **TOTAL FAT:** 15 g   **CARBS:** 28 g   **DIETARY FIBER:** 2 g   **PROTEIN:** 28 g

SEAFOOD CIOPPINO with SAFFRON, TOMATO, and FENNEL BROTH

In my cooking at Miraval, I like my dishes to have bold, clean flavors, and to highlight the character of each ingredient. In this seafood stew, I decided to roast the mushrooms and fennel separately instead of simmering them in the broth. I use the roasted veggies as a final garnish, which adds a nice layer of texture as well as flavor. **SERVES 6**

2 Tbsp. Miraval Oil Blend (see page 118) in a spray bottle

Kosher salt to taste

Freshly ground black pepper to taste

12 fresh mussels

12 large shrimp, peeled and deveined

6 sea scallops

1 fennel bulb, top trimmed, cored, and sliced

1 c. quartered white or cremini mushrooms

1½ c. Saffron, Tomato, and Fennel Broth (recipe follows)

¼ tsp. chopped fresh thyme

¼ tsp. chopped fresh oregano

¼ tsp. chopped fresh flat Italian parsley

Heat a large skillet over high heat and spray with Miraval Oil Blend. Season the seafood with kosher salt and freshly ground black pepper. Add the mussels to the skillet, and then arrange the shrimp and scallops in the pan as well. Leave to cook until nicely browned on the first side, 3 to 4 minutes. Once brown on the first side, turn over and brown other side.

Heat the oven to 375°F. Arrange the fennel and mushrooms on a baking sheet, spray everything lightly with Miraval Oil Blend, and sprinkle with salt and pepper. Roast in oven for 10 to 15 minutes until fennel and mushrooms are soft and lightly browned. Transfer the seafood from the skillet to six wide bowls. Spoon ¼ cup of broth into center of each bowl. Add the roasted fennel and mushrooms and sprinkle with some finely chopped thyme, oregano, and flat Italian parsley. Serve right away.

CALORIES: 120   **TOTAL FAT:** 2.5 g   **CARBS:** 16 g   **DIETARY FIBER:** 4 g   **PROTEIN:** 11 g

SAFFRON, TOMATO, AND FENNEL BROTH

MAKES 4 CUPS

½ tsp. extra-virgin olive oil

1 bulb fennel, ends trimmed, chopped

1 Tbsp. minced shallots

1 Tbsp. minced garlic

1 c. white wine

2 whole black peppercorns

1 tsp. saffron threads

3 c. tomato juice

¼ tsp. kosher salt

⅛ tsp. freshly ground black pepper

Heat a saucepan over medium heat and add the olive oil. Add the fennel, shallots, and garlic. Sauté about 2 minutes, taking care not to burn the garlic. Add the white wine, peppercorns, and saffron to the saucepan.

Simmer until the wine is reduced by half and then add in tomato juice. Bring to a boil and simmer for about 15 minutes. Pour the mixture into a blender and blend until smooth. Season with the salt and pepper. The broth will keep in the refrigerator for up to a week.

SERVING SIZE: ¼ cup **CALORIES:** 20 **TOTAL FAT:** 0 g **CARBS:** 4 g **DIETARY FIBER:** 1 g
PROTEIN: 1 g

PAN-SEARED GROUPER with SWISS CHARD, ROASTED TOMATOES, and VEAL REDUCTION

I really like to pair mild fish, such as this grouper, with a garnish of veal reduction. The drizzle of reduced veal stock provides a meaty, savory accent that makes the dish special. If you aren't able to include it, don't worry—the combination of roasted tomatoes and Swiss chard is plenty flavorful. A good substitute for the grouper would be mahi mahi or sea bass. **SERVES 4**

1 pint cherry tomatoes

1 tsp. olive oil

Kosher salt to taste

Freshly ground black pepper to taste

4 tsp. fresh oregano leaves

1 tsp. white balsamic vinegar

Veal stock reduction, optional (see page 122)

1½ tsp. Miraval Oil Blend (see page 118)

3 c. chopped Swiss chard leaves (remove the stems first)

4 four-ounce pieces grouper or other firm white fish, skin removed

Heat the oven to 425°F. Line a rimmed baking sheet with parchment. Toss the cherry tomatoes with the olive oil and season with salt and pepper. Spread on the baking sheet and roast until the tomatoes start to split and collapse and the skins are starting to brown, about 25 minutes. Slide the tomatoes and all their juices into a bowl. Gently fold in 2 teaspoons of the oregano and the vinegar. Taste and adjust the salt and pepper. Keep warm.

If you're using the veal stock, simmer it in a small saucepan until slightly thickened; keep warm.

Heat ½ teaspoon Miraval Oil Blend in a large sauté pan over medium-high. Add the chard and cook, tossing frequently, until wilted and tender, 5 to 6 minutes. Keep warm. Season with a pinch of salt just before serving.

Season both sides of the grouper with salt and pepper. Heat 1 teaspoon of the Miraval Oil Blend in a heavy sauté pan over high, add the fish, and quickly sear for 2 to 3 minutes on each side.

Arrange a bed of Swiss chard on each plate, nestle a piece of grouper on top, and then spoon over some warm roasted tomatoes. If using the veal broth, drizzle a spoonful over each. Finish by sprinkling on the remaining oregano. Serve immediately.

CALORIES: 150   **TOTAL FAT:** 4.5 g   **CARBS:** 5 g   **DIETARY FIBER:** 2 g   **PROTEIN:** 23 g

HALIBUT with SPICY GREENS, ISRAELI COUSCOUS, and PONZU BROTH

I enjoy cooking with halibut because it has a mild flavor and a very firm but moist texture that won't fall apart when you cook it. In this dish, the fish pairs nicely with the bright, citrusy flavors of the ponzu broth, and the whole dish is accented by a spicy sauce in which I cook the greens. Both the ponzu broth and sauce can be made days ahead, making this a nice dish to serve for a dinner party. **SERVES 4**

2 c. baby spinach leaves, washed and dried

2 heads baby bok choy, steamed and then roughly chopped

¼ c. Spicy Sauté Sauce (recipe follows)

2 c. cooked Israeli couscous, kept warm

½ c. Ponzu Broth (recipe follows)

4 four-ounce skinless halibut filets

Kosher salt to taste

Freshly ground black pepper to taste

¼ tsp. Miraval Oil Blend (see page 118)

Heat a large sauté pan over high, add the spinach and steamed bok choy, and toss to wilt the spinach. Add the Spicy Sauté Sauce and toss to combine and heat through, 2 to 3 minutes. Take from the heat, set aside, and keep warm.

Put the cooked couscous in a saucepan with the ponzu broth and simmer until hot. Keep warm.

Season each side of the halibut with a little salt and pepper. Heat a medium sauté pan on high heat and add the oil. Cook just until no longer translucent inside, 2 or 3 minutes per side.

Divide the bok choy and spinach among four shallow bowls. Spoon the couscous and broth on top of the greens and arrange the halibut on top. Serve right away.

CALORIES: 340   **TOTAL FAT:** 10 g   **CARBS:** 30 g   **DIETARY FIBER:** 3 g   **PROTEIN:** 33 g

PONZU BROTH

MAKES 2 CUPS

⅔ c. fresh orange juice

½ c. soy sauce or tamari

¼ c. miso paste (white or red)

Grated zest and juice from 2 oranges

Grated zest and juice from 1 lemon

Grated zest and juice from 2 limes

Put the orange juice, soy sauce, and miso in a mixing bowl and whisk together until the miso dissolves. Add the citrus juices and zest and let sit for 30 minutes at room temperature. Strain. The sauce will keep in the refrigerator for two weeks.

SERVING SIZE: 2 ounces **CALORIES:** 70 **TOTAL FAT:** 1 g **CARBS:** 9 g **DIETARY FIBER:** 1 g **PROTEIN:** 6 g

SPICY SAUTÉ SAUCE

MAKES 1 CUP

½ c. soy sauce or tamari

¼ c. toasted sesame oil

¼ c. sambal chili sauce

Whisk the ingredients together in a small bowl. The sauce will keep in the refrigerator for up to 1 month.

SERVING SIZE: 2 tablespoons **CALORIES:** 70 **TOTAL FAT:** 7 g **CARBS:** 1 g **DIETARY FIBER:** 0 g **PROTEIN:** 2 g

MUSSELS IN THAI COCONUT SAUCE

A hallmark of Thai cuisine is the balance between sweet, spicy, salty, and sour flavors. When everything is in the right proportion, the food will have a vibrant flavor that makes you want to take the next bite. That balance between essential flavors is also a hallmark of our cuisine at Miraval, and this easy mussel dish is a perfect example. **SERVES 4**

4 slices artisan-style whole-wheat bread (for crostini)

¼ tsp. Miraval Oil Blend (see page 118)

24 mussels, preferably from Prince Edward Island (scrubbed and rinsed)

3 Tbsp. thinly sliced shallots

2 Tbsp. chopped garlic

⅔ c. white wine

½ c. coconut milk

2 Tbsp. sambal oelek

2 Tbsp. fresh lime juice

⅓ c. tomato, seeded and diced

1 Tbsp. thinly sliced fresh Thai basil

Pinch kosher salt

Freshly ground black pepper to taste

1 Tbsp. fresh chopped cilantro

Heat the oven to 350°F. Cut the whole-wheat bread into quarters and toast in oven until crisp, 7 to 8 minutes.

Heat a large sauté pan over medium-high, add the Miraval Oil Blend, and add the mussels. Sauté the mussels for a few seconds and then add the shallots and garlic and sauté for another 45 seconds.

Add the white wine, coconut milk, sambal, and lime juice. Simmer for 1 minute, add the Thai basil and tomato, and continue to simmer for 2 minutes. Lightly season with salt and pepper to taste. The mussels should be open by now and ready to serve. Divide the mussels between four bowls, sprinkle with the fresh cilantro, and serve right away.

PLATING: Have four bowls ready. Place three mussels in each bowl, ladle your sauce over the top, place the crostini on the side, and serve.

CALORIES: 240   TOTAL FAT: 9 g   CARBS: 18 g   DIETARY FIBER: 2 g   PROTEIN: 16 g

SEAFOOD MEDLEY with SAFFRON FETTUCCINE in GARLIC WHITE-WINE SAUCE

Saffron and tomato are fantastic flavor partners for seafood, especially shellfish such as scallops and shrimp. I like to use fettuccine that's flavored with saffron, but you could use plain pasta and add a small pinch of saffron to your sauce when you add the garlic. You can make the sauce up to a few hours ahead and just reheat as you assemble the final dish. **SERVES 4**

½ tsp. olive oil

¼ c. finely diced red onion

4 large sea scallops, cut in half crosswise

8 oz. white fish, such as cod or halibut, cut into small chunks

4 shrimp, peeled and deveined

2 c. cooked saffron fettuccine noodles (see basic pasta on page 131)

4 Tbsp. chopped tomatoes

4 c. baby spinach leaves

1 c. Garlic White-Wine Sauce (recipe follows)

Heat a large sauté pan over high heat and add the oil to the pan when hot. Add the onion and cook until soft and starting to brown, about 4 minutes. Add the scallops and let them cook, without moving, until nicely seared on one side, about 1 minute. Turn the scallops, add the fish and shrimp to the pan, and continue to cook until all the seafood is just cooked through. Transfer everything to a bowl or plate and keep warm.

Return the skillet to the heat and add the pasta, tomato, and spinach to the pan. Cook, tossing frequently, until the pasta is heated through, the tomatoes are softening, and the spinach has wilted. Add the sauce and cook another minute, tossing frequently, until the ingredients are hot. Divide the pasta and sauce among four pasta bowls, top with the seafood and any accumulated juices, and serve right away.

CALORIES: 230 **TOTAL FAT:** 3 g **CARBS:** 28 g **DIETARY FIBER:** 2 g **PROTEIN:** 18 g

GARLIC WHITE-WINE SAUCE

MAKES ABOUT 1 CUP

¼ tsp. Miraval Oil Blend (see page 118)

¼ c. yellow onion, finely chopped

1 tsp. chopped garlic

¼ c. dry white wine

½ tsp. chopped fresh thyme leaves

1 c. plain rice milk

Pinch of salt and pepper

In a medium saucepan, heat the Miraval Oil Blend over medium. Add the onions and cook, stirring frequently, until they are soft and translucent, about 3 minutes. Add the garlic and cook 30 seconds. Then add the wine and thyme and simmer until reduced to a glaze.

Add the rice milk and continue to simmer until reduced by about half and the sauce has a nice consistency. Season to taste with salt and pepper.

SERVING SIZE: ¼ cup   **CALORIES:** 50   **TOTAL FAT:** 1 g   **CARBS:** 8 g   **DIETARY FIBER:** 0 g
PROTEIN: 0 g

LENTIL PORTOBELLO ROLL-UPS with FETA and TOMATILLO, LIME, and ROASTED CORN SALSA

These roll-ups are essentially small burritos, filled with hearty ingredients and topped with a zingy salsa that serves as a contrast to the earthiness of the lentils and portobello mushrooms. **SERVES 6**

½ onion, thinly sliced

½ c. diced potatoes

1 c. sliced portobello mushrooms

2 cloves garlic, minced

½ c. pink lentils

4 c. vegetable stock (see page 116)

2 c. fresh trimmed and washed spinach

2 Tbsp. chopped fresh oregano

¼ tsp. dried chili flakes

½ c. crumbled feta cheese

6 twelve-inch flour tortillas, warmed

2 c. Tomatillo, Lime, and Roasted Corn Salsa (recipe follows)

Spray a deep-sided sauté pan lightly with nonstick cooking spray. Add the onions and sauté over medium-high, stirring frequently, until the onions are soft and fragrant, about 5 minutes. Add the potatoes, mushrooms, and garlic and cook another 10 minutes, stirring frequently. (Don't let the garlic burn.)

Add the lentils and stock and cook until the lentils and potatoes are fully cooked, another 25 minutes or so. Remove the pan from the stove and fold in the spinach, oregano, and chili flakes. The lentil-vegetable mix should not be dry, but it also should not be too wet or it will make the tortilla soggy. If necessary, drain off any excess. Add the feta and fold to mix well.

Heat oven to 425°F.

On the stove, heat a dry sauté pan over low heat and warm each tortilla. Cover the hot tortillas with a cloth napkin or clean dish towel or just place them in a plastic bag so they don't dry out.

Spray a medium baking dish with nonstick cooking spray. Place about 2 tablespoons of the lentil mix in the lower part of each tortilla, fold in the sides, and then roll them up. Carefully place the tortilla roll-ups seam-side down in the baking dish. Bake on the center rack in the heated oven for about 20 minutes or until the tortilla roll-ups are crispy and golden brown. Serve with tomatillo salsa.

CALORIES: 420　**TOTAL FAT:** 9 g　**CARBS:** 70 g　**DIETARY FIBER:** 8 g　**PROTEIN:** 17 g

TOMATILLO, LIME, AND ROASTED CORN SALSA

SERVES 6

¼ habanero chili, stemmed, seeded, and minced

½ scallion, chopped

1 medium onion, chopped

6 tomatillos, husked, rinsed, and chopped

1 Tbsp. chopped fresh oregano

1 clove minced garlic

2 Tbsp. chopped fresh cilantro

Kosher salt to taste

Freshly ground black pepper to taste

½ c. nopales, cooked and diced (optional)

½ c. fresh corn kernels, toasted in a dry skillet until golden brown

Juice of 1 lime

Put the habanero, scallion, onion, tomatillos, oregano, garlic, and cilantro in a food processor and pulse until you have a nice chunky consistency.

Transfer to a bowl and season generously with salt and pepper. Add the nopales (if using), the corn, and lime juice; stir to blend, and taste for seasoning. Set aside until ready to use.

SERVING SIZE: ¼ cup   **CALORIES:** 35   **TOTAL FAT:** 0 g   **CARBS:** 7 g   **DIETARY FIBER:** 2 g
PROTEIN: 1 g

TOFU CURRY with JASMINE RICE

"Curry" is a term that can mean different things depending on what cuisine we're talking about. My recipe here gets its inspiration from Thai cooking via some spicy Thai red curry paste, which is available in a jar in the Asian food section. If you can get real Thai basil for this recipe, you'll be rewarded by a more exotic and sweet perfume than the more familiar Italian basil. But either will be delicious. **SERVES 4**

1 c. uncooked jasmine rice

1 (12-oz.) package firm tofu, drained and cut into ½-inch cubes

2 Tbsp. Miraval Oil Blend (see page 118)

2 c. haricot verts or other slender green beans, cut in half

1 eggplant, peeled and cut into ½-inch cubes (you should have around 3½ cups)

1 large red bell pepper, cored, seeded, cut into julienne strips

1 c. vegetable stock (see page 116)

2 Tbsp. red curry paste

3 Tbsp. tamari (gluten-free soy sauce) or soy sauce

2 tsp. brown sugar

½ c. thinly sliced Thai basil

2 tsp. grated lime zest

Cook the rice according to the directions on the package, timing it so that the rice will be hot when you're ready to serve the curry.

Pat the drained tofu dry with a paper towel, pressing lightly until most of the liquid is absorbed. Heat a large pan on medium-high heat, add 1 tablespoon of the Miraval Oil Blend, and when hot, add the tofu. Sauté for 3 to 4 minutes until lightly browned; transfer to a plate and keep warm.

Return the pan to the heat, add the remaining tablespoon of Miraval Oil Blend, and add the haricot verts, eggplant, and red bell peppers. Sauté for 4 minutes, stirring occasionally, and then add the vegetable stock and red curry paste. Stir for about 30 seconds to blend. Add the tamari and brown sugar and cook for another 5 minutes. Add the tofu back to the pan along with half the Thai basil and stir to mix together.

Divide the cooked, hot rice between four wide bowls. Ladle on about 1½ cups of the tofu curry and garnish with rest of the Thai basil and fresh lime zest.

CALORIES: 350   **TOTAL FAT:** 8 g   **CARBS:** 58 g   **DIETARY FIBER:** 8 g   **PROTEIN:** 13 g

HUNAN BARBECUE TOFU STIR-FRY

One of tofu's many good qualities is that it soaks up the flavors of the ingredients around it. In this case, it takes on all the flavors of the zingy Asian barbecue sauce that I use to finish this dish. At Miraval, I like to use brown rice with my stir-fries because of the added nutritional value and because I like the nutty flavor and slightly chewy texture. **SERVES 4**

8 oz. firm tofu, cut into 1-inch cubes

1 tsp. canola oil

1 medium stalk celery, cut at an angle into ½-inch slices

2 oz. snow peas, trimmed

4 oz. baby carrots, boiled or steamed until just barely tender

1 medium red bell pepper, cored, seeded, and cut into large dice

½ c. Hunan Barbecue Sauce (recipe follows)

2 oz. vegetable stock (see page 116)

2 baby bok choy, halved and boiled or steamed until just barely tender, and then chopped roughly on an angle

2 c. hot, cooked brown rice

1 small red radish, sliced

¼ c. sliced scallion

Pat the drained tofu dry with a paper towel, pressing lightly until most of the liquid is absorbed. Heat the oil in a large sauté pan over medium-high heat. When hot, add the celery, snow peas, and carrots and sauté for 4 to 5 minutes, until they are cooked through and hot but still crisp.

Add the bell peppers and tofu and toss together with the vegetables. Add the Hunan Barbecue Sauce, cook for a minute to heat through, tossing the mixture to coat evenly.

Add the vegetable stock and let the mixture simmer for 2 minutes. Add the bok choy at the very end and toss to just warm. To serve, place a half-cup of hot cooked rice in the middle of each plate, spoon the vegetable mix over the top, and garnish with the radish slices and scallions.

CALORIES: 300   **TOTAL FAT:** 4.5 g   **CARBS:** 56 g   **DIETARY FIBER:** 7 g   **PROTEIN:** 10 g

HUNAN BARBECUE SAUCE

MAKES ABOUT ½ CUP

¼ tsp. canola oil

½ tsp. minced fresh ginger

½ tsp. minced garlic

2 Tbsp. rice wine vinegar

2 Tbsp. light soy sauce

½ c. hoisin sauce

⅓ c. orange juice

1½ tsp. curry powder

¼ c. plus 1 Tbsp. water

1 tsp. cornstarch

Heat the oil in a medium saucepan over medium-high heat, and then add the ginger and garlic. Sauté 2 to 3 minutes, but do not brown.

Add the vinegar, soy sauce, hoisin sauce, orange juice, curry powder, and ¼ cup of the water. Let this mixture come to a boil, stirring occasionally. In a small separate bowl, mix the cornstarch and 1 tablespoon of water. Add this to the saucepan and stir constantly until sauce comes back to a boil.

Once it has boiled, turn down and let simmer, stirring occasionally, until the sauce thickens. Strain the sauce through a medium strainer and serve.

SERVING SIZE: 2 tablespoons   **CALORIES:** 100   **TOTAL FAT:** 1.5 g   **CARBS:** 20 g
DIETARY FIBER: 1 g   **PROTEIN:** 1 g

ROASTED VEGETABLE and SWEET POTATO STRUDELS

Wrapping anything up in phyllo pastry is a great way to make it special. Here I take a mix of colorful vegetables and herbs, roast them to bring out their sweetness, and then roll them in the pastry to create a strudel. At Miraval, I will often pair the strudel with other elements, such as pork tenderloin, but it's delicious and hearty enough to eat as a vegetarian main dish. **MAKES 9 INDIVIDUAL STRUDELS**

FILLING

2 medium sweet potatoes, peeled and cut into 2-inch sticks

1 medium bunch asparagus, stem ends removed, then cut in half lengthwise and crosswise to make short, thin pieces

1 medium carrot, peeled, cut into 2-inch sticks or 1 cup baby carrots

1 medium zucchini, cut into 2-inch sticks

½ tsp. extra-virgin olive oil

¼ tsp. kosher salt

⅛ tsp. freshly ground black pepper

1 Tbsp. chopped mixed fresh herbs (such as a mix of Italian parsley, oregano, thyme, and basil)

1 c. teardrop or cherry tomatoes, halved

MAKE THE FILLING: Heat the oven to 450°F.

Place the sweet potatoes, asparagus, carrot, and zucchini on a baking sheet. Toss the vegetables with the olive oil and season with the salt, pepper, and herbs. Roast the vegetables for 10 minutes, or until lightly browned and moisture is noticeable. Remove the vegetables from the oven and transfer to a clean dish.

Reduce the oven temperature to 425°F and line a baking sheet with parchment.

PHYLLO

9 sheets phyllo dough

Olive oil spray

3 Tbsp. chopped mixed fresh herbs (such as a mix of Italian parsley, oregano, thyme, and basil)

FOR THE PHYLLO: Gently lay one piece of phyllo dough on a clean cutting board. Lightly mist with olive oil spray. Sprinkle with 1 teaspoon of mixed herbs. Repeat with phyllo and herbs to make two more layers. You will have three layers of phyllo. (Keep remaining phyllo covered with a damp towel.)

Cut the rectangle into thirds lengthwise so you have three long strips. On each rectangle pile ⅓ cup of the vegetables. Lay three tomatoes on top of vegetables. Fold in the sides of the dough and lift the bottom of the dough over the vegetables. Begin to gently roll up the strudel. You will be making a cylinder, like a burrito. Repeat with remaining phyllo and vegetables to make a total of nine strudel rolls.

Place the strudels on a baking sheet lined with parchment paper. Lightly mist the top and sides of each strudel with olive oil spray. Bake the strudel for 10 to 12 minutes, or until golden brown.

CALORIES: 110   **TOTAL FAT:** 1.5 g   **CARBS:** 20 g   **DIETARY FIBER:** 3 g   **PROTEIN:** 3 g

RISOTTO with FRESH HERBS, SHIITAKES, and ASPARAGUS

Risotto may seem like a "restaurant dish"—something that's too tricky to make well at home—but in fact, the method is quite easy and quick. The key is buying the right type of rice, which will develop a nice creamy consistency but still stay al dente. I often make a version of risotto without any garnish—just the finishing of Parmesan—to serve as a side dish to simple meats and fish, but when you add ingredients such as the mushrooms and asparagus in this dish, risotto becomes a meal in itself. **SERVES 4**

½ tsp. olive oil

4 large shiitake mushrooms, stems cut off and discarded, sliced

8 spears asparagus, trimmed and cut into 1-inch lengths

2 c. vegetable stock (see page 116) or canned vegetable broth

¼ tsp. Miraval Oil Blend (see page 118) or canola oil

1 Tbsp. chopped yellow onion

¼ tsp. minced garlic

½ c. arborio or carnaroli rice

½ c. dry white wine

½ tsp. minced fresh parsley

¼ tsp. minced fresh oregano

¼ tsp. minced fresh thyme

Heat the olive oil in a medium sauté pan over high. Add the shiitakes and sauté for about 1 minute. Add the asparagus, season lightly with salt and pepper, and continue to cook the vegetables until they are lightly browned and tender. Set aside and keep warm.

Put the vegetable stock in a small saucepan and bring to a simmer over medium-high heat. Remove from the heat and cover to keep warm until ready to use.

Heat the Miraval Oil Blend in a medium saucepan or deep skillet over medium-high heat. Add the onion and garlic and cook, stirring, until fragrant, about 45 seconds. Add the rice and cook, stirring, for 1 minute. Add the wine and cook until reduced by half, 1 to 1½ minutes.

¾ tsp. kosher salt

¾ tsp. freshly ground black pepper

1 Tbsp. grated Parmigiano-Reggiano

Add 1½ cups of the hot stock and stir well. Cook at a low simmer, stirring occasionally, until nearly all the stock is absorbed, 6 to 7 minutes. Add the additional ½ cup stock and cook, stirring occasionally, for 2 minutes. Add the herbs, shiitakes, and asparagus, stir well, and cook for 2 minutes. Add the salt and pepper, stir well, and cook until all the liquid is absorbed, 1 to 1½ minutes. Add the cheese, stir well, and cook until melted, 30 seconds.

Remove the pan from the heat and serve immediately.

SERVING SIZE: ½ cup   **CALORIES:** 160   **TOTAL FAT:** 1.5 g   **CARBS:** 27 g   **DIETARY FIBER:** 3 g **PROTEIN:** 4 g

Miraval Basics, Accents, and Side Dishes

VEGETABLE STOCK

If you spend some time making a big batch of this stock and stashing it in the freezer, you'll be ahead of the game when it comes time to make many soups and sauces.

MAKES ABOUT 1 QUART

2 qt. water

3 c. roughly chopped yellow onion

2 c. roughly chopped tomato

1½ c. roughly chopped celery

1½ c. roughly chopped carrots

½ c. roughly chopped cremini or shiitake mushrooms

2 tsp. black peppercorns

5 sprigs fresh thyme

Put all the ingredients into a stockpot and bring to a boil. Reduce the heat to a simmer and cook uncovered for 2 hours. The stock will reduce by quite a bit.

Strain the stock through a fine mesh strainer or colander lined with cheesecloth. Cool to room temperature and then divide into smaller containers. Store in the refrigerator up to five days or the freezer up to one month.

SERVING SIZE: ¼ cup   **CALORIES:** 25   **TOTAL FAT:** 0 g   **CARBS:** 6 g   **DIETARY FIBER:** 16 g   **PROTEIN:** 1 g

THICKENED VEGETABLE STOCK

We use this ingredient when we want to create body in a dish without adding fat.

MAKES 1⅔ CUPS

3 c. vegetable stock (see page 116)

4 Tbsp. cornstarch

3 Tbsp. cold water

Bring the stock to a boil in a small saucepan. In a small bowl, whisk together the cornstarch and water to make a slurry. Whisk the slurry into the simmering stock, a bit at a time, whisking to blend thoroughly after each addition. Once all the slurry has been added, simmer until the stock is thickened and heavily coats the back of a spoon.

Let cool to room temperature, transfer to an airtight container, and keep in the refrigerator for up to two weeks.

SERVING SIZE: ½ cup   **CALORIES:** 20   **TOTAL FAT:** 0 g   **CARBS:** 5 g   **DIETARY FIBER:** 1 g
PROTEIN: 0 g

MIRAVAL OIL BLEND

We use this blended oil regularly in the Miraval kitchens, and we call for it in many of the recipes in this book. The canola can withstand high cooking temperatures, and the olive oil adds flavor. **MAKES 1 CUP**

¾ c. canola oil

¼ c. extra-virgin olive oil

Combine the oils and transfer to a mister or spray bottle, which will allow you to dispense small amounts.

SERVING SIZE: 1 tablespoon   **CALORIES:** 144   **TOTAL FAT:** 17.5 g   **CARBS:** 0 g
DIETARY FIBER: 0 g   **PROTEIN:** 0 g

BALSAMIC REDUCTION

Choose a decent, but not artisan-quality, balsamic vinegar for this; you don't want one that includes caramel coloring or other additives. The only trick to making this reduction—which you can drizzle on vegetables, meat, poultry, fish . . . anything, really—is to not over-reduce it, or it can get bitter and sticky. Test the consistency by dipping a spoon into the reduction. When it coats the back of the spoon nicely, it's ready.

MAKES ABOUT ¾ CUP

2 cups balsamic vinegar

Put the vinegar in a medium saucepan and bring to a low boil over medium heat. Reduce the heat and simmer gently until the vinegar has reduced by slightly more than half, 25 to 30 minutes; it should be fairly syrupy. Cool and then store in a tightly closed container in the refrigerator. The reduction will last for months.

SERVING SIZE: 2 tablespoons **CALORIES:** 14 **TOTAL FAT:** 0 g **CARBS:** 3 g **DIETARY FIBER:** 0 g **PROTEIN:** 0 g

MARINARA SAUCE

MAKES 3 CUPS

½ tsp. extra-virgin olive oil

2 Tbsp. minced garlic

32 oz. canned stewed tomatoes and their juices

2 Tbsp. roughly chopped fresh basil

½ tsp. sugar or agave syrup

½ tsp. kosher salt

⅛ tsp. freshly ground black pepper

Heat the oil in a medium pot over medium-high heat. Add the garlic and cook, stirring, until starting to brown, 45 seconds. Add the remaining ingredients and bring to a boil. Reduce the heat and simmer until the tomatoes are very tender and start to break apart and the liquid is reduced by about one-quarter in volume, 14 to 15 minutes.

Transfer to a blender and blend on high speed until smooth. Use as directed in recipes.

The sauce will keep refrigerated in an airtight container for up to four days. It also can be frozen in an airtight container for up to one month.

SERVING SIZE: ¼ cup   CALORIES: 50   TOTAL FAT: 0 g   CARBS: 10 g   DIETARY FIBER: 3 g   PROTEIN: 1 g

BASIC CHICKEN STOCK

MAKES 2 QUARTS

1 bay leaf

1 tsp. fresh thyme leaves

2 Tbsp. whole black peppercorns

1 c. yellow onions, chopped

½ c. celery ribs, chopped
(no leaves)

3 lb. chicken bones or 3
carcasses, thoroughly washed,
excess fat removed

3 qt. cold water

In a large stockpot, combine all ingredients. Add enough cold water to cover the bones and the vegetables. Bring contents to a boil, reduce heat, and simmer uncovered for 4 hours.

Using a slotted spoon, skim off any impurities such as foam and fat throughout the cooking process.

Strain stock through a colander lined with cheesecloth or through a fine mesh strainer, discarding bones and vegetables.

Use stock immediately or cool down in an ice bath. Once the stock is cool (below 40°F), store in the refrigerator in an airtight container for up to one week or freeze for about one month.

SERVING SIZE: 1 cup **CALORIES:** 60 **TOTAL FAT:** 1 g **CARBS:** 11 g **DIETARY FIBER:** 2 g **PROTEIN:** 3 g

VEAL STOCK

MAKES 1 GALLON

5 lb. veal knuckle bones, cut

1½ c. burgundy or cabernet
sauvignon wine

1 c. yellow onion, peeled
and chopped

1 c. carrots, peeled and chopped

1 c. celery, chopped (no leaves)

⅓ c. tomato paste

1 tsp. fresh thyme sprigs

1 bay leaf

1 tsp. whole black peppercorns

1½ gal. cold water

Preheat the oven to 400°F.

Rinse the bones and place in a roasting pan. Place the pan in the oven and roast the bones for about 1 hour, or until a deep brown color. Using tongs, carefully remove the bones from pan and place in a large bowl.

Add the wine to the hot roasting pan and scrape off the sediments from the bottom of pan for additional flavor. Reserve this mixture.

Heat a large stockpot over medium heat and add the vegetables. Sauté, stirring occasionally to prevent scorching, until vegetables are softened, 3 to 5 minutes. Stir in the tomato paste and red wine mixture. Stir to fully incorporate. Add the thyme, bay leaf, peppercorns, bones, and water. Bring to a boil, reduce heat, and simmer for 24 hours.

Using a slotted spoon, skim off any impurities such as foam and fat throughout the cooking process. As the stock cooks, check the water level. You may need to add additional cold water to maintain the liquid volume in the stockpot. Toward the end of the cooking period, let the stock reduce by about one-third of the original amount.

Strain stock through a colander lined with cheesecloth or a fine mesh strainer, discarding bones and vegetables.

Use stock immediately or cool down in an ice bath. Store in the refrigerator in an airtight container for up to one week or freeze in large zip-top bags for about one month.

SERVING SIZE: 1 cup **CALORIES:** 70 **TOTAL FAT:** 1 g **CARBS:** 9 g **DIETARY FIBER:** 0 g **PROTEIN:** 4 g

BASIC ROASTED VEGETABLES

MAKES 4 SERVINGS

8 oz. baby carrots, scrubbed clean, stems trimmed

4 oz. broccolini

½ tsp. Miraval Oil Blend (see page 118)

¼ tsp. kosher salt

¼ tsp. freshly ground black pepper

Preheat the oven to 375°F.

Bring a pot of water to a boil. Add the carrots and cook until they start to become tender, 4 minutes. Add the broccolini and cook for 1 minute.

Transfer the vegetables to a baking dish and toss with the oil, salt, and pepper. Place in the oven and roast until tender and starting to brown, 8 minutes. Serve immediately.

SERVING SIZE: ½ cup **CALORIES:** 35 **TOTAL FAT:** 0.5 g **CARBS:** 7 g **DIETARY FIBER:** 2 g **PROTEIN:** 1 g

BASIC SAFFRON RICE

MAKES 6 CUPS

5 c. water

1 Tbsp. saffron thread

2 c. basmati rice (dry)

Fill a medium-sized sauce pot with the water and bring just to a simmer. Add saffron and the 2 cups of rice. Reduce the flame to a medium heat and cook for 16 minutes. Pull off heat, give it a good stir, and cover the pot with tinfoil. Steam rice for 5 minutes. Serve immediately or refrigerate and serve later.

SERVING SIZE: per ⅓ cup   CALORIES: 60   TOTAL FAT: 0 g   CARBS: 14 g   DIETARY FIBER: 1 g
PROTEIN: 1 g

BALSAMIC-ONION RELISH

SERVES 4

1 Tbsp. oil

½ small red onion, cut into small dice

¼ c. balsamic vinegar

Heat the oil in a small skillet over medium-high heat. Add the onions and cook until caramelized and soft, 7 to 9 minutes. Add the balsamic vinegar and cook until the onions are evenly coated and the vinegar is only on the onions, not in the pan. Set aside until cool and use to garnish soups, salads, and main dishes.

SERVING SIZE: 1 teaspoon **CALORIES:** 50 **TOTAL FAT:** 3.5 g **CARBS:** 6 g **DIETARY FIBER:** 0 g **PROTEIN:** 0 g

BASIC CARAMELIZED RED ONIONS

MAKES 4 SERVINGS

1 medium-size red onion

¼ tsp. Miraval Oil Blend (page 118)

Take one whole onion, cut it in half, peel off outer skin layer, and cut root off each end. Julienne the onion as thinly as possible, spray ¼ tsp. of Miraval Oil Blend in the pan, place the julienne onion in a medium-size sauté pan; and sauté for 5 to 6 minutes, until caramelized.

These caramelized onions can be used on a pizza or tossed in with a salad of your choice.

SERVING SIZE: 1 tablespoon **CALORIES:** 15 **TOTAL FAT:** 0 g **CARBS:** 3 g **DIETARY FIBER:** 0 g **PROTEIN:** 0 g

PARMESAN and OLIVE CRACKERS

MAKES 4 WAFERS

4 Tbsp. shredded Parmesan

1 tsp. finely chopped kalamata olives

Pinch dried basil

Heat the oven to 350°F. Line a baking sheet with a silicone baking mat. Divide the cheese into 4 piles on the baking mat, spaced far apart. Using your fingers or a fork, spread the cheese evenly, and then sprinkle with the olives and the dried basil.

Cook in the hot oven until melted into a lacy wafer that's lightly golden brown, 5 to 7 minutes. Let cool for a few minutes and then carefully slide off the silicone mat with a spatula. Add about a tablespoon of these crackers to soup.

SERVING SIZE: 1 wafer **CALORIES:** 25 **TOTAL FAT:** 1.5 g **CARBS:** 0 g **DIETARY FIBER:** 0 g **PROTEIN:** 2 g

QUINOA FETTUCCINE with SEASONAL VEGETABLES

SERVES 4

8 oz. carrots, cut into julienne strips

8 oz. julienned zucchini

8 oz. julienned yellow squash

8 oz. dry quinoa linguine

Heat a medium sauté pan over medium heat and coat with cooking spray. Add the carrots, zucchini, and yellow squash. Sauté for 2 minutes, just to soften. Meanwhile, bring a large pot of salted water to a boil, cook the pasta according to the package, and drain well. Toss the vegetables in a mixing bowl with the hot pasta and serve right away.

SERVING SIZE: ½ cup   CALORIES: 240   TOTAL FAT: 2 g   CARBS: 56 g   DIETARY FIBER: 6 g   PROTEIN: 7 g

PARMESAN-SAGE WHIPPED SWEET POTATOES

SERVES 4

4 medium sweet potatoes (about 2 lb.)

3 Tbsp. nonfat milk

½ tsp. chopped fresh sage

¼ cup grated Parmesan

⅛ tsp. kosher salt

Heat oven to 400°F.

Place the sweet potatoes on a small baking sheet or dish. Roast until very tender and the skin starts to split, 45 to 50 minutes. Remove the potatoes from the oven, let cool for 5 minutes, and pull the skins off. Put into a mixing bowl and mash with a fork or sturdy whisk.

Heat the milk in a small saucepan until just warm, add the chopped sage, and then fold into the potatoes. Add salt and half the Parmesan. Mix together well, sprinkle the remaining Parmesan over the top, and serve.

SERVING SIZE: ½ cup **CALORIES:** 220 **TOTAL FAT:** 1.5 g **CARBS:** 46 g **DIETARY FIBER:** 7 g **PROTEIN:** 6 g

BASIC FLATBREAD DOUGH

MAKES 12 SERVINGS

1 c. warm water, not above 110°F

1 Tbsp. active dry yeast

¼ c. extra-virgin olive oil, plus 1 tsp. to grease the bowl

¼ c. honey or agave syrup

2 c. whole-wheat flour

1½ c. semolina flour

1 tsp. kosher salt

Combine the water, yeast, ¼ cup of the oil, and the honey in the bowl of an electric mixer fitted with a dough hook and let the mixture sit until foamy, 5 to 10 minutes.

Stir together the flour, semolina, and salt in a medium bowl.

With the machine on low speed, slowly add the flour mixture ½ cup at a time to the yeast mixture. After all dry ingredients have been added, continue to mix the dough on low speed for 5 minutes.

Lightly oil a large bowl with 1 tsp. oil and place the dough inside. Cover the dough with plastic wrap and let sit until almost double in size, about 1 hour.

Turn out the dough onto a lightly floured work surface and divide into 12 equal portions. One at a time, roll out each portion to ¼-inch in thickness.

Use as directed in the recipe.

SERVING SIZE: 1 flatbread (¹⁄₁₂ of recipe) CALORIES: 170 TOTAL FAT: 4 g CARBS: 29 g DIETARY FIBER: 3 g PROTEIN: 5 g

BASIC PASTA

To make your own saffron pasta for the Seafood Medley with Saffron Fettuccine on page 102, add two tablespoons of saffron threads while kneading the dough. **SERVES 8**

2 c. semolina flour, plus more for flouring the work surface

2 eggs

1 tsp. plus 1 Tbsp. salt

4 Tbsp. water

4 tsp. extra-virgin olive oil

MIX THE DOUGH: Mound the semolina on a large wooden cutting board or marble work surface, and make a crater in the center of the mound. Break the eggs into the crater, and then add 1 teaspoon of the salt, the water, and 3 teaspoons of the olive oil. Beat the mixture with a small whisk or fork. Slowly draw in the semolina with the whisk until it's fully incorporated and starts to have a solid form.

KNEAD THE DOUGH: Flour your work surface with some semolina. Knead the dough by holding it in place with the palm of one hand and stretching it away from itself with your other hand. Fold it together and repeat the process until the dough is elastic and shows a "pebbly" surface when the ball is broken in half. Cover the dough and let it rest for 30 minutes in the refrigerator.

ROLL THE DOUGH: Cut the ball of dough into three equal pieces. Form these pieces into rectangular shapes to be passed through a manual pasta machine or with a rolling pin. Make sure to flour your work surface so that the pasta doesn't stick. You want to roll the dough out to a half-inch thickness. As you roll the dough, it may become sticky, so lightly flour the sheet of dough before rolling again. Once you've rolled the pasta into sheets, cut it into long strips or your desired shape.

TO COOK: Bring a pot of water to a boil, and add 1 Tbsp. of salt. Add the pasta and cook for 3 to 4 minutes or until tender. Drain pasta and toss with the remaining olive oil. Serve immediately with a dish from this book or as is with a little salt and pepper.

CALORIES: 185 **TOTAL FAT:** 3 g **CARBS:** 30 g **DIETARY FIBER:** 1.5 g **PROTEIN** 7 g

POTATO GNOCCHI

SERVES 4

2 c. smashed boiled potato

1 Tbsp. cornstarch

1 c. unbleached all-purpose flour

½ c. vegetable stock (see page 116)

2 tsp. extra-virgin olive oil plus 1 tsp. for sautéing

1 tsp. roasted garlic puree (optional)

2 tsp. kosher salt

1 tsp. black pepper

Pinch of kosher salt and pepper to taste (when sautéing the gnocchi in the pan)

Bring a large pot of salted water to a boil.

Using a wooden spoon or a fork, mix the mashed potatoes with the cornstarch and flour until the flour is mostly absorbed. Add the stock, 2 teaspoons of the olive oil, roasted garlic if using, salt, and pepper and continue to mix until you have a dough-like consistency.

On a lightly floured work surface, roll the dough into a rope about the thickness of your index finger. Cut it into 1-inch lengths. Drop the gnocchi a few at a time into the boiling water and cook for 2 to 3 minutes or until they float. Scoop out the gnocchi, drain, and put into a bowl to keep warm while you finish cooking all the dough.

Heat a large skillet over medium-high, add the last teaspoon of olive oil, and add the gnocchi. Season with salt and pepper and sauté until crisp. Serve right away.

SERVING SIZE: 1 gnocchi **CALORIES:** 210 **TOTAL FAT:** 4 g **CARBS:** 39 g **DIETARY FIBER:** 2 g **PROTEIN:** 4 g

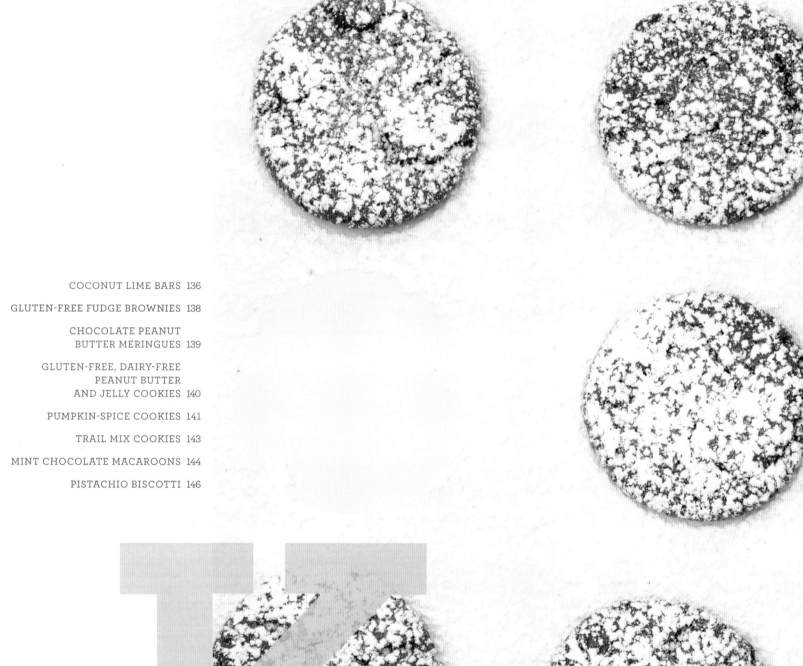

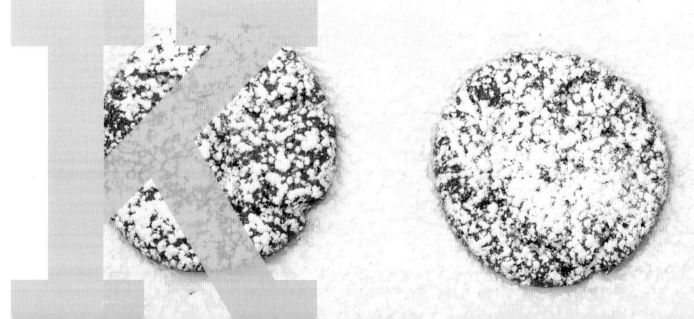

Kim's Cookies, Bars, and Baked Goods

COCONUT LIME BARS

Everybody loves this kind of slightly fancy bar cookie, especially my version with fresh lime juice and lime zest—although, the classic lemon version is pretty great, too. These are easy to make—just press the crust into the pan—but they're delectable enough to serve as a dessert for guests or to bring to a cookie swap. I use coconut oil instead of butter in the crust, which has a wonderful flavor and no cholesterol. You can add toasted coconut to the top for garnish if desired. **MAKES 16 TWO-INCH BARS**

CRUST

1½ c. graham-cracker crumbs

2 Tbsp. coconut oil

2 Tbsp. melted butter

2 Tbsp. granulated sugar

Pinch salt

FILLING

3 Tbsp. granulated sugar

2 Tbsp. cornstarch

1 can (14-oz.) low-fat sweetened condensed milk

1 egg

⅓ c. fresh lime juice

¼ c. low-fat coconut milk

1 tsp. finely grated lime zest

MAKE THE CRUST: Heat the oven to 350°F. Grease an 8-inch x 8-inch baking pan with nonstick cooking spray. In a small bowl, combine the graham-cracker crumbs, oil, butter, sugar, and salt. Press the crust into the bottom of the prepared pan. Bake for 10 minutes or until lightly brown, remove from oven, and let cool at room temperature.

MAKE THE FILLING: In a medium bowl, whisk together the sugar and cornstarch. Whisk in the condensed milk, egg, lime juice, coconut milk, and zest, whisking until smooth. Pour the filling over the prepared crust.

Bake for 25 minutes until lightly set in the center, taking care not to over-cook. Let cool at room temperature for 30 minutes and then transfer to the refrigerator to cool for 1 hour or until well chilled. Cut into 16 squares.

SERVING SIZE: 1 two-inch bar **CALORIES:** 174 **TOTAL FAT:** 5 g **CARBS:** 27 g **DIETARY FIBER:** .5 g **PROTEIN:** 3 g

GLUTEN-FREE FUDGE BROWNIES

A lot of modern baking recipes don't call for sifting dry ingredients because when you're dealing with ordinary flour, it's not usually necessary. But I've found that the flours and starches that are used in gluten-free baking do need sifting in order to avoid clumping and to be sure they're completely blended together. **MAKES 16 BROWNIES**

¼ c. melted unsalted butter or coconut oil

1½ c. granulated sugar

1 whole egg

2 egg whites

1 tsp. pure vanilla extract

¾ c. all-purpose gluten-free flour (look for brands such as Bob's Red Mill, King Arthur, and Arrowhead Mills) or sorghum flour

½ c. unsweetened natural cocoa powder

2 Tbsp. tapioca flour

2 Tbsp. potato starch

½ tsp. xanthan gum

Pinch kosher salt

¼ tsp. baking powder

½ c. semisweet chocolate chips

Heat the oven to 350°F and grease an 8-inch x 8-inch pan with nonstick cooking spray.

In a medium bowl, whisk the butter and sugar until combined. Add the whole egg, egg whites, and vanilla extract and mix until smooth.

In another bowl, sift together the all-purpose gluten-free flour, cocoa powder, tapioca flour, potato starch, xanthan gum, salt, and baking powder. Add the wet ingredients to the dry and mix with a rubber spatula until just combined. Fold in the chocolate chips; do not overmix or the brownies will be tough.

Spread the batter in the prepared pan. Bake for 30 to 35 minutes, or until the edges are crisp and pull away from the sides of the pan. (Take care not to overcook, or brownies will be dry and crumbly.) Let cool to room temperature and then cut into 16 squares.

SERVING SIZE: 1 brownie **CALORIES:** 170 **TOTAL FAT:** 6 g **CARBS:** 31 g **DIETARY FIBER:** 2 g **PROTEIN:** 2 g

CHOCOLATE PEANUT BUTTER MERINGUES

I love these cookies because they're true crowd-pleasers, and if you make them using dairy-free chocolate chips (so no milk chocolate or white chocolate), they're not only gluten-free, but dairy-free, too . . . not to mention lower in fat than most cookies. Feel free to use walnuts if you prefer them to pecans. **MAKES 30 COOKIES**

3 egg whites

⅔ c. granulated sugar

¼ tsp. pure vanilla extract

¼ c. peanut butter (preferably organic)

¼ c. mini semisweet chocolate chips

¼ c. chopped pecans

Heat the oven to 200°F and line a baking sheet with kitchen parchment.

In a stand mixer fitted with a whip attachment, whip the egg whites until they form soft peaks. Once at soft peak, slowly add the granulated sugar and then add the vanilla.

Drop spoonfuls of peanut butter throughout the meringue and sprinkle the chocolate chips all over. Using a rubber spatula, gently fold the peanut butter and chocolate chips into the meringue, leaving streaks of peanut butter throughout. (It's okay if there are a few small chunks of peanut butter.) Take care not to deflate the meringue.

Drop spoonfuls of meringue (about ¾-ounce or 1½ tablespoons) onto the prepared baking sheet and sprinkle with the chopped pecans. Bake for about 45 minutes. Test for doneness by removing one cookie from the oven, letting it cool for 2 minutes, and then testing to see if the outside is crispy and the inside is slightly soft. Let cool at room temperature on the baking sheet and store in an airtight container.

SERVING SIZE: 1 cookie **CALORIES:** 45 **TOTAL FAT:** 2 g **CARBS:** 27 g **DIETARY FIBER:** 0 g **PROTEIN:** 1 g

GLUTEN-FREE, DAIRY-FREE PEANUT BUTTER and JELLY COOKIES

These easy-to-make cookies are a lot like a traditional thumbprint cookie, with a dollop of colorful jam in the center, but they are of course lighter than a flour-based cookie and happen to be vegan. I use an organic, natural-style peanut butter, but in a pinch, you could use a grocery-store type. **MAKES 2 DOZEN COOKIES**

1½ c. organic peanut butter

½ c. raw cane sugar

½ c. light brown sugar

1½ tsp. Ener-G Egg Replacer (egg substitute)

2 Tbsp. water

¼ c. strawberry or raspberry jelly or jam

Heat the oven to 350°F. Line a baking sheet with parchment and spray with nonstick cooking spray.

In a mixer fitted with the paddle attachment, cream together the peanut butter and the cane and brown sugars until smooth. In a separate bowl, mix the egg substitute and water together until smooth, and then add it to the peanut butter mixture.

Scoop about 1 tablespoon of the dough and roll into a ball with your hands. Use the back of a ½-teaspoon measuring spoon to make an indentation in the top of each dough ball. Drop ¼ teaspoon jelly into the center of each cookie. Repeat with the rest of the dough.

Bake until very lightly browned and the jelly is set in the center, 10 to 12 minutes. Remove from oven and let cool at room temperature.

SERVING SIZE: 1 cookie **CALORIES:** 120 **TOTAL FAT:** 8 g **CARBS:** 10 g **DIETARY FIBER:** 1 g **PROTEIN:** 4 g

PUMPKIN-SPICE COOKIES

These homey cookies are so perfect for fall and winter—the combination of pumpkin and spices says "holiday," and because the recipe makes a lot of cookies, it's a good one for those office parties and school functions that inevitably fill our end-of-year calendars. I like to use a mix of all-purpose and whole-wheat flour for more nutrition and a nice nuttiness. **MAKES 24 COOKIES**

2 Tbsp. butter, softened

2 Tbsp. prune puree

1 c. brown sugar

¾ c. canned pumpkin

¼ c. molasses

1 egg

1 egg white

1 tsp. vanilla extract

1½ c. unbleached all-purpose flour

½ c. whole-wheat flour

½ tsp. baking soda

1 tsp. baking powder

1 tsp. cinnamon

½ tsp. allspice

½ tsp. ginger

Pinch of kosher salt

Heat the oven to 350°F. Spray a baking sheet with nonstick cooking spray and set aside.

In a bowl of a stand mixer fitted with a paddle attachment, cream together the softened butter, prune puree, and brown sugar. Add the canned pumpkin, molasses, egg, egg white, and vanilla and continue to mix until smooth.

In a separate bowl, sift together the flours, baking soda, and baking powder and add the cinnamon, allspice, ginger, and salt. Add the dry ingredients to the mixer and mix on low speed just until incorporated. Scoop spoonfuls of dough onto the baking sheet, leaving about 2 inches of space between the balls of dough. (They will spread slightly during cooking.) Bake for 12 to 14 minutes, until puffed and slightly golden around the edges. Cool at room temperature.

SERVING SIZE: 1 cookie **CALORIES:** 100 **TOTAL FAT:** 1 g **CARBS:** 20 g **DIETARY FIBER:** 1 g **PROTEIN:** 2 g

TRAIL MIX COOKIES

Making these cookies is really easy—you use a simple "drop" method—and I never hesitate to give them to our daughter because they're so full of good ingredients. You get whole grains from the oats, fantastic healthful oils from the seeds and nuts, vitamins and anti-oxidants from the fruit, and of course lots of fiber. The recipe makes quite a few cookies, but they freeze well if you seal them tightly in a freezer bag. **MAKES ABOUT 3 DOZEN COOKIES**

4 Tbsp. butter, softened

½ c. light or dark brown sugar

¼ c. raw cane sugar

½ c. honey or agave nectar

2 egg whites

1 c. all-purpose flour

½ tsp. baking soda

¼ tsp. kosher salt

2 c. rolled oats

½ c. mixed seeds and/or nuts (pumpkin, sunflower, etc.)

½ c. mixed dried fruit (cranberries, cherries, blueberries, etc.)

¼ c. mini semisweet chocolate chips

Heat the oven to 350°F and line a baking sheet with kitchen parchment.

In a stand mixer fitted with the paddle attachment, cream the butter, brown sugar, and cane sugar together until smooth. Add the honey and egg whites, scrape down the sides of the bowl using a rubber spatula, and continue to mix for another minute.

In a small bowl, whisk together the flour, baking soda, and salt. Add this mixture and the oats to the ingredients in the mixer and continue mixing until just combined. Last, add the seeds, dried fruit, and chocolate chips. Scoop 1-tablespoon portions onto the prepared baking sheet, leaving about 1 inch between the cookies. Bake until the cookies are lightly browned and they release from the parchment, 8 to 10 minutes. Remove from oven and cool on a wire rack.

SERVING SIZE: 1 cookie   **CALORIES:** 96   **TOTAL FAT:** 2 g   **CARBS:** 17 g   **DIETARY FIBER:** 1 g
PROTEIN: 2 g

MINT CHOCOLATE MACAROONS

Meringue is such a wonderful thing—fat-free, delicate, chewy, and crunchy at the same time. Making a good meringue takes a little attention, especially when you're adding ingredients such as the cocoa and mint candies in this recipe. The key is to fold in the ingredients very, very gently so that you don't deflate all the volume that you've whipped into the egg whites. I like to use a large rubber spatula. Cut the spatula through the meringue to the bottom of the bowl and then, as you bring it back up, fold the meringue back onto itself. Turn the bowl a bit and repeat until you've moved through the whole mixture. **MAKES 2 DOZEN COOKIES**

2 c. powdered sugar

¼ c. unsweetened cocoa powder

5 egg whites

¼ c. chopped chocolate mint candies (such as Andes)

Heat the oven to 350°F. Line a baking sheet with parchment and spray with nonstick cooking spray.

Sift the powdered sugar and cocoa powder into separate bowls and set aside. In a stand mixer fitted with a whip attachment, whip the egg whites until soft peaks form. Slowly add the powdered sugar, a half cup at a time, taking care not to add the sugar too quickly, which would deflate the egg whites. Once the sugar has been added, add the cocoa powder at low speed, and then fold in the chopped candies using a rubber spatula.

Transfer the batter to a piping bag (no tip needed). (You can also use a large zip-top plastic bag with one corner snipped off.) Pipe out quarter-sized mounds of batter on the prepared baking sheet. Bake until the cookies are puffed to about double their size and a crisp shell has formed on the top, 12 to 15 minutes. They should release easily from the parchment. Remove from the oven and cool to room temperature.

SERVING SIZE: 1 cookie **CALORIES:** 50 **TOTAL FAT:** 0.5 g **CARBS:** 11 g **DIETARY FIBER:** 0 g **PROTEIN:** 1 g

PISTACHIO BISCOTTI

Biscotti are a sophisticated cookie that I like to serve as an accompaniment to simple desserts, such as ice cream or sorbet. I also will pair a biscotti and a cup of coffee as a mid-morning pick-me-up in the pastry kitchen. Biscotti are excellent keepers if you store them in an airtight container. **MAKES 24 COOKIES**

1 c. unbleached all-purpose flour

1 tsp. baking powder

⅓ c. evaporated raw cane sugar, plus 1 Tbsp. for sprinkling

½ c. almond flour

⅓ c. whole pistachios (shells removed) with skin on

½ tsp. vanilla extract

½ tsp. almond extract

1 Tbsp. apple juice

3 large egg whites, plus 1 egg white, lightly beaten, for brushing on the top

Heat the oven to 350°F. Line a baking sheet with parchment and spray with nonstick cooking spray.

Sift the flour with the baking powder and put in a medium bowl. Add the sugar, almond flour, and pistachios. Combine the vanilla extract, almond extract, apple juice, and 3 egg whites. Gradually add the wet ingredients into the dry and mix for 1 minute.

Lightly flour the work surface and roll the dough into a long rope. Brush the top with the lightly beaten egg white and sprinkle the 1 tablespoon sugar on the top of the loaf. Bake for 20 to 25 minutes or until browned on top. Let the biscotti sit at room temperature for 1 hour.

Cut the baked loaf on an angle into 24 diagonally shaped biscotti. Place the biscotti on a cut side in a single layer on a baking sheet and bake at 350°F until golden brown, approximately 10 minutes. Cool the biscotti on a wire rack.

SERVING SIZE: 1 cookie   **CALORIES:** 50   **TOTAL FAT:** 1 g   **CARBS:** 9 g   **DIETARY FIBER:** 0 g   **PROTEIN:** 2 g

KIM'S COOKIES, BARS, AND BAKED GOODS   147

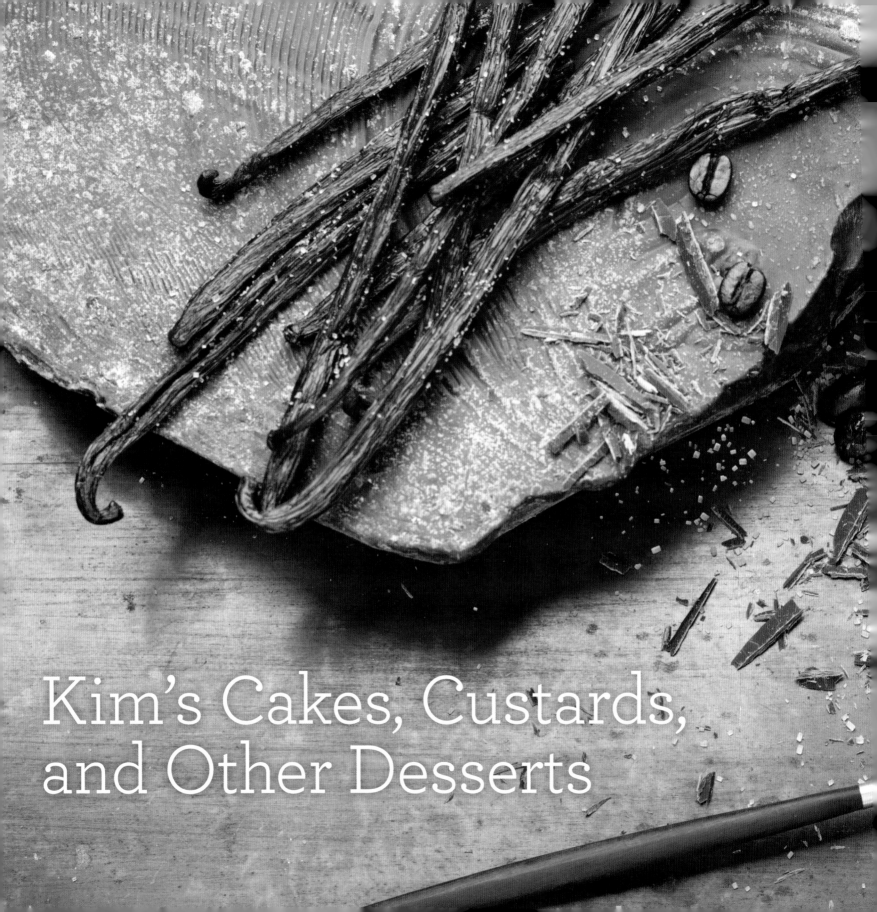

Kim's Cakes, Custards, and Other Desserts

OLD-FASHIONED RASPBERRY CAKE

This homey and delicious cake gets its moist, tender crumb from a mix of butter and fruit puree (either prune or banana), which adds richness without the fat. I like to keep things simple by just serving squares of the cake with a dusting of powdered sugar, but you could pair it with some fresh raspberries or a raspberry puree as a pretty sauce, too.

MAKES ONE 8-INCH X 8-INCH CAKE (16 SERVINGS)

1 Tbsp. unsalted butter, softened at room temperature

2 Tbsp. prune puree or mashed ripe banana

⅔ c. raw cane sugar

1 whole egg

1 egg white

½ tsp. pure vanilla extract

1¼ c. unbleached all-purpose flour

1¼ tsp. baking powder

½ tsp. baking soda

½ tsp. ground cinnamon

Pinch kosher salt

⅔ c. low-fat buttermilk

½ c. fresh raspberries, rinsed and drained, or ½ cup frozen berries

Powdered sugar, for dusting

Heat the oven to 350°F. Spray an 8-inch x 8-inch cake pan with nonstick cooking spray. Dust the insides (base and sides) with flour and tap to remove excess.

With an electric mixer, cream together the butter, prune puree, and sugar on medium speed for 4 minutes, until well blended. Add the egg, egg white, and vanilla and beat until well blended.

Put the flour, baking powder, baking soda, cinnamon, and salt in a bowl and whisk to blend. Add the flour mixture to the butter mixture, alternating with the buttermilk, beginning and ending with flour mixture; mix well after each addition. Gently fold in the raspberries with a rubber spatula.

Spoon the batter into the prepared pan. Bake for 20 to 25 minutes or until a wooden pick inserted in the center of the cake comes out clean. Let the cake cool in pan for 5 minutes. To serve, run a knife around edges and turn pan over onto a serving plate. Cut into 16 squares and dust with powdered sugar.

SERVING SIZE: 1 piece (¹⁄₁₆ of cake) **CALORIES:** 90 **TOTAL FAT:** 1 g **CARBS:** 18 g **DIETARY FIBER:** 1 g **PROTEIN:** 2 g

GLUTEN-FREE APPLECAKE

I love having a gluten-free version of this homey dessert. The cake is so versatile that I can serve it perfectly plain as an afternoon snack or dress it up with some caramel sauce or sautéed apples and serve it for dessert to Miraval guests. I prefer to use Granny Smith apples because I like the tartness, but any nice apple you have on hand will be just fine.

MAKES ONE 8-INCH X 8-INCH CAKE, SERVES 16

½ c. cream cheese

⅓ c. butter, softened

1 c. plus 2 Tbsp. granulated sugar

1 egg

1 egg white

1 tsp. vanilla extract

½ c. all-purpose gluten-free flour

¼ c. sorghum flour

1 Tbsp. plus 1 tsp. tapioca starch

1 Tbsp. plus 1 tsp. potato starch

¼ tsp. xanthan gum

1 tsp. baking powder

Pinch salt

1 Tbsp. cinnamon

2 c. Granny Smith apples, peeled, cored, and cut in medium dice

Heat the oven to 350°F and spray an 8-inch x 8-inch baking pan with nonstick cooking spray.

In a stand mixer fitted with a paddle attachment, cream together the cream cheese and softened butter. Add 1 cup of granulated sugar and continue to beat until smooth, scraping down the sides of the bowl occasionally with a rubber spatula. Next add the egg, egg white, and vanilla extract and continue to mix for another 30 seconds.

In a separate bowl, sift together the gluten-free flour, sorghum flour, tapioca starch, potato starch, xanthan gum, baking powder, and salt. Add the dry ingredients to the mixer and mix until incorporated. Set aside.

In another small bowl, mix together the 2 tablespoons sugar and 1 tablespoon cinnamon. Remove one tablespoon of the cinnamon-sugar and set aside. Toss the diced apples in the cinnamon-sugar mixture that's left in the bowl and then fold them into the cake batter.

Pour the apple batter into the baking pan and sprinkle with the reserved cinnamon-sugar. Bake for 30 minutes or until golden brown and cake springs back when touched in the center.

Cut into 16 squares and serve warm. This dessert can be served on its own or with a scoop of vanilla ice cream or low-fat caramel sauce.

SERVING SIZE: 1 piece (¹⁄₁₆ of cake)   **CALORIES:** 180   **TOTAL FAT:** 7 g   **CARBS:** 27 g
DIETARY FIBER: 1 g   **PROTEIN:** 2 g

BROWN SUGAR PINEAPPLE CAKE with MACADAMIA NUT ICE CREAM and CARAMEL SAUCE

I love to take classic desserts and give them a modern update. I give our Miraval version of this upside-down cake a fresh flavor twist by pairing it with macadamia nut ice cream. I also give the cake a healthful update by swapping out butter for coconut oil in the pineapple topping. Take care when you flip the cake onto the serving plate—the sugary juices can be hot! **MAKES ONE 10-INCH CAKE, SERVES 16**

½ c. coconut oil

1 c. brown sugar

12 slices of fresh pineapple (sliced ¼-inch thick)

¾ c. unbleached all-purpose flour

1 tsp. baking powder

¼ tsp. kosher salt

4 eggs, separated

1 c. granulated sugar

1 tsp. almond extract

1 Tbsp. melted butter or coconut oil

Caramel Sauce (recipe follows) and Macadamia Nut Ice Cream (recipe follows)

Heat the oven to 350°F. Distribute the coconut oil and the brown sugar evenly over the bottom of a 10-inch cake pan. Place the sliced pineapple on top of the oil/sugar mixture. Set aside.

In a separate bowl, sift together the flour, baking powder, and salt. Set aside.

In a stand mixer fitted with the whip attachment, whip the egg yolks and ½ cup of the sugar until thick and pale yellow (about 1 minute). Mix the almond extract and melted butter into the yolk mixture and then fold in the flour mixture by hand using a rubber spatula.

In a separate bowl, whip the egg whites until they form soft peaks and then slowly add the remaining ½ cup of sugar. Continue to whip until medium to stiff peaks form. Gently fold the whipped egg whites into the flour/yolk base. Spread the batter evenly over the pineapple slices in the cake pan.

Bake for 35 minutes until set and the cake springs back when tapped lightly in the center. Cool the cake for 10 minutes and then invert it onto a serving plate. Cut into 16 slices and serve warm with macadamia nut ice cream and low-fat caramel sauce.

CARAMEL SAUCE

MAKES ABOUT 2 CUPS

1½ c. sugar

½ c. water

½ tsp. lemon juice

¾ c. heavy cream

¼ c. milk

In a small saucepan, bring the sugar, water, and lemon juice to a boil. Meanwhile, heat the cream and milk in a separate pan until scalding. Remove from the heat and set aside. Cook the sugar until it becomes amber in color, remove from the heat, and pour in the hot milk/cream. (The mixture will bubble rapidly, so be careful.) Stir until smooth. Strain through a fine mesh strainer and transfer to a container. Store in the refrigerator until ready to use (can be stored in refrigerator for up to seven days).

MACADAMIA NUT ICE CREAM

MAKES 4 CUPS

½ c. macadamia nuts

2 c. nonfat milk

¼ c. heavy cream

½ c. half-and-half

1 can low-fat sweetened condensed milk

2 vanilla beans, split lengthwise

1 Tbsp. hazelnut liqueur (such as Frangelico)

Heat the oven to 350°F. Spread the macadamia nuts on a baking sheet and toast in the oven for 12 minutes or until golden brown. Remove and let cool at room temperature for about 20 minutes. Put the nuts in a food processor and grind until very fine.

Put the milk, cream, half-and-half, and condensed milk in a bowl and whisk until mixed. Scrape the seeds from the vanilla beans and add them to the mixture, whisking to distribute them. (They may want to stay in clumps at first.)

Stir the grounds nut and liqueur into the mixture. Freeze in an ice-cream maker according to manufacturer's instructions.

SERVING SIZE: 1 slice of cake, 2 oz. of ice cream, and 2 tablespoons of sauce
CALORIES: 220   **TOTAL FAT:** 9 g   **CARBS:** 35 g   **DIETARY FIBER:** 1 g   **PROTEIN:** 3 g

PASTEL DE TRES LECHES

I try to make every dessert at Miraval a celebration, which is why I don't skimp on the ingredients that make the dish truly special. In this traditional Mexican cake, I find ways to cut back on some of the fat in the cake itself so that I can still frost it with real whipped cream. **MAKES 16 INDIVIDUAL CAKES OR ONE 8-INCH X 8-INCH CAKE**

¼ c. unsalted butter

1 c. raw cane sugar

¼ c. unsweetened applesauce

3 large whole eggs

4 large egg whites

2 tsp. pure vanilla extract

1½ c. all-purpose flour

1 tsp. baking powder

½ tsp. ground anise

1 c. nonfat milk

½ c. 2 percent milk

6 oz. (½ can) evaporated skim milk

¼ c. granulated sugar

2 Tbsp. Amaretto liqueur

½ c. heavy whipping cream

Heat the oven to 350°F. Spray 16 six-ounce ramekins or an 8-inch x 8-inch baking dish (such as a Pyrex brownie pan) with nonstick cooking spray.

In a stand mixer fitted with the paddle attachment, cream the butter and the raw sugar until fluffy. With the mixer running on low, add the applesauce, whole eggs, egg whites, and vanilla. Mix until thoroughly combined. Sift together the flour, baking powder, and ground anise and sprinkle into the batter. Mix until just blended. Pour the batter into the prepared baking pan or ramekins.

Bake for 15 minutes if in ramekins or 25 minutes if in pan, until a toothpick inserted into the center of the cakes comes out clean. Take the cakes from the oven and poke all over with a fork or skewer to make holes so the milk mixture will absorb nicely.

Combine nonfat, 2 percent, and evaporated milk, 1 tablespoon of the granulated sugar, and the Amaretto. Put the milk mixture into a small saucepan and heat until the sugar is dissolved. Pour the milk mixture evenly over the cake and chill at least 2 hours.

Whip the heavy cream and the remaining 3 tablespoons granulated sugar. Just before serving, frost the top of the cake or ramekins with whipped cream.

SERVING SIZE: 1 individual cake or ¹⁄₁₆ of 8-inch x 8-inch cake **CALORIES:** 200 **TOTAL FAT:** 7 g **CARBS:** 28 g **DIETARY FIBER:** 0 g **PROTEIN:** 5 g

GLUTEN-FREE CHIFFON CAKE

Chiffon cakes were all the rage in the 1940s and '50s, and they are making a comeback now. Both moist and airy, they are a lovely style of cake that can be dressed up in so many ways. The version that I've created at Miraval is even more modern because it's wheat-, dairy-, and soy-free. Serve it simply on its own, with some berries and a touch of whipped cream, or frosted with a glaze or whipped frosting. **MAKES 16 SERVINGS**

⅓ c. almond, hazelnut, or grape-seed oil

½ c. water

4 egg yolks

1 tsp. pure vanilla extract

1 tsp. almond extract

1¼ c. gluten-free all-purpose flour

1¼ c. granulated sugar

½ tsp. xanthan gum

4 egg whites

Heat the oven to 350°F. Spray the bottom of a 9-inch springform pan with nonstick cooking spray and then line the bottom of the pan with a circle of kitchen parchment cut to fit. Spray the parchment and the insides of the pan.

Combine the oil, water, and yolks in a mixer and whip until foamy. Add the vanilla and almond extracts. Add the flour and 1 cup of the sugar and beat until smooth.

Sprinkle in the xanthan gum and whip until the mixture forms a thick, ribbon-like consistency. Transfer batter to a medium-size bowl.

In another bowl, whip the egg whites until they form medium peaks and slowly add the remaining ¼ cup of sugar. Gently fold the whipped egg whites into the batter.

Pour mixture into the prepared pan. Bake for 20 to 30 minutes or until the cake is golden brown and springs back when touched. Serve plain or with berries or frosting.

SERVING SIZE: 1 slice (¹⁄₁₆ of cake)   **CALORIES:** 150   **TOTAL FAT:** 6 g   **CARBS:** 23 g
DIETARY FIBER: 1 g   **PROTEIN:** 3 g

RICH GLUTEN-FREE MOLTEN CHOCOLATE CAKE

Gluten-free baking often requires using several different types of flours and starches in one recipe, and it's important to be sure they are thoroughly blended. In this recipe, I use a whisk to combine the sorghum and tapioca flours, the potato starch, and the xanthan gum, along with the powdered sugar, to make sure my dry ingredients are homogenous.

MAKES 10 INDIVIDUAL CAKES

¼ c. plus 2 Tbsp. sorghum flour

1 Tbsp. tapioca flour

1 Tbsp. potato starch

¼ tsp. xanthan gum

1½ c. powdered sugar

8 Tbsp. butter or Smart Balance

8 oz. 64 percent dark chocolate

1 banana

3 eggs

3 yolks

1 tsp. vanilla extract

2 Tbsp. Grand Marnier

Berries, for serving

Heat the oven to 425°F. Spray 10 four-ounce ramekins with nonstick baking spray.

In a medium bowl, whisk together the sorghum flour, tapioca flour, potato starch, xanthan gum, and powdered sugar. Set aside. Melt the butter and chocolate together in the microwave or in a double boiler.

In a separate bowl, mash the banana until almost smooth. Add the eggs, egg yolks, vanilla, and Grand Marnier and incorporate into the chocolate-butter mixture. Add the flour mixture and whisk until smooth. Divide the batter between the prepared ramekins and bake for about 15 minutes, until the sides of the cake are set and the center is slightly jiggly. Run a knife around the edge of the ramekins and invert onto serving plates. Serve hot with fresh berries.

SERVING SIZE: 1 cake **CALORIES:** 334 **TOTAL FAT:** 19 g **CARBS:** 37 g **DIETARY FIBER:** 3 g **PROTEIN:** 5 g

GLUTEN-FREE MOCHA CAKE

I love this cake because it's such an all-purpose, go-to cake. Sometimes I'll serve it simply with just a dusting of powdered sugar, and other times I'll plate it with a scoop of gelato and a drizzle of sauce to really dress it up. And the real beauty is that it freezes nicely, so you can make two cakes, serve one now, and save the other for last-minute entertaining. **MAKES TWO 9-INCH CAKES, 16 SERVINGS EACH**

3 c. sugar

1½ c. 1- or 2-percent milk

2 eggs

2 yolks

6 oz. (12 Tbsp.) melted unsalted butter

1½ tsp. vanilla extract

1 tsp. coffee extract

3 c. gluten-free all-purpose flour (such as Bob's Red Mill or King Arthur)

1 c. unsweetened natural cocoa powder

1 tsp. xanthan gum

1½ tsp. baking powder

1½ tsp. baking soda

½ tsp. kosher salt

1½ c. boiling water

Heat the oven to 350°F. Spray two 9-inch springform pans with nonstick cooking spray and then line the bottom of each with a circle of parchment paper. Spray again and set aside.

In the bowl of a stand mixer fitted with the paddle attachment, combine the sugar, milk, eggs, yolks, melted butter, vanilla, and coffee extracts. Mix on medium speed until blended.

In a separate bowl, sift together the gluten-free flour, cocoa powder, xanthan gum, baking powder, and baking soda. Slowly add dry ingredients, including salt, into mixer with the wet ingredients. Mix for 30 seconds or until batter is smooth. With the mixer on low speed, slowly add the boiling water and mix just until blended.

Pour the batter into the prepared pans and bake for 40 minutes or until the cake is set and springs back when pressed in the middle. Remove the pans from the oven and cool to room temperature and then unmold from springform. Serve immediately or cool in the refrigerator until ready to use. The cakes can be frozen, tightly wrapped in freezer-proof plastic wrap, for up to one month.

SERVING SIZE: 1 slice (1/16 of cake)   **CALORIES:** 186   **TOTAL FAT:** 5 g   **CARBS:** 33 g
DIETARY FIBER: 2 g   **PROTEIN:** 3 g

LOW-FAT LEMON-BUTTERMILK POUND CAKE

One of the beauties of this pound cake is that using low-fat buttermilk not only cuts down on fat but it also promotes a super-tender cake. Acidic ingredients, such as buttermilk or yogurt—and of course the lemon juice in the recipe—help to "cut" the gluten in regular flour. Less gluten means a more tender crumb and a more delicious pound cake. **MAKES TWO 9-INCH X 5-INCH LOAF CAKES (32 SERVINGS)**

½ c. unsalted butter, softened at room temperature

3 c. sugar

½ c. applesauce

5 eggs

½ c. low-fat buttermilk

½ c. lemon juice

1 tsp. vanilla extract

1 tsp. lemon zest

3 c. unbleached all-purpose flour

½ tsp. baking powder

½ tsp. kosher salt

½ c. nonfat milk

Powdered sugar, for sprinkling (optional)

Heat the oven to 350°F. Spray two 9-inch x 5-inch loaf pans with nonstick cooking spray. Dust inside with flour and tap out the excess.

Using a stand mixer fitted with the paddle attachment, cream together the butter and sugar. Add the applesauce and beat until smooth. Then add in the eggs one at a time, scraping down the sides of the bowl with a rubber spatula after each addition. Next pour in the buttermilk and lemon juice and add the vanilla and zest.

In a separate bowl, sift together the flour and baking powder. Add the salt. Gradually add the flour to the butter-egg mixture (with the mixer on low), alternating with the milk, until the batter is smooth. Take care not to overmix.

Pour the batter into the prepared pan and bake for 1 hour or until a toothpick inserted into the center comes out clean. Let cool at room temperature for 15 minutes before inverting onto a serving plate. Sprinkle with powdered sugar, if you like.

SERVING SIZE: 1 slice (¹⁄₁₆ of loaf)   **CALORIES:** 320   **TOTAL FAT:** 8 g   **CARBS:** 58 g
DIETARY FIBER: 1 g   **PROTEIN:** 5 g

KEY LIME ICE CREAM

A scoop of this tangy-creamy treat makes a wonderful finish to a meal, and the ice cream is also lovely served alongside a slice of simple cake or some fresh strawberries and kiwi slices. Fresh key limes aren't easy to find, but bottled key lime juice is available in stores and will work just fine in this recipe. **MAKES 3 CUPS, SIX ½-CUP SERVINGS**

1½ c. nonfat milk

¼ c. heavy cream

¼ c. half-and-half

1 (14-oz.) can nonfat sweetened condensed milk

½ c. key lime juice

⅛ tsp. xanthan gum

Put all the ingredients into a large bowl and whisk until smooth. Freeze in an ice-cream maker according to the manufacturer's instructions.

SERVING SIZE: ½ cup   CALORIES: 310   TOTAL FAT: 13 g   CARBS: 41 g   DIETARY FIBER: 0 g   PROTEIN: 8 g

BLACKBERRY CHOCOLATE-CHUNK GELATO

Blackberries are so delicious but can be slightly troublesome to work with. First, they have a short growing season and therefore are not always available fresh. And second, they are very seedy, and unlike the small seeds in, say, raspberries, these guys are big! That is why a puree is an ideal destination for a blackberry. You can use frozen berries, and you'll strain out all the seeds.

To make a blackberry puree, pile them into a blender or food processor (make sure they are thawed, if using frozen), process until smooth, and then push through a mesh strainer, using the back of a spoon or a rubber spatula. For 1 cup puree, start with about 2¼ cups berries. **MAKES ABOUT 4 CUPS, EIGHT ½-CUP SERVINGS**

3 c. 2 percent milk

5 egg yolks

¾ c. granulated sugar

1 c. blackberry puree

¼ tsp. xanthan gum

½ c. chopped 64 percent dark chocolate chunks

In a saucepan, heat the milk until it comes to a gentle simmer. Meanwhile, combine the egg yolks and sugar in a bowl and slowly whisk the hot milk into the egg mixture. Return the milk-egg mixture to the stove on medium-low heat, stirring constantly with a heat-proof rubber spatula until it begins to thicken; the custard will coat the back of a spoon. (Take care not to overheat because the eggs will scramble.) You can test with a thermometer; it should reach 165°F.

Remove the custard from the heat, strain through a fine mesh sieve, and cool. Stir in the blackberry puree and chill in the refrigerator for at least 4 hours. Once chilled, whisk in the xanthan gum. Freeze according to your ice-cream maker's instructions. While the gelato is mostly frozen but still soft, stir in the chocolate chunks. Transfer to an airtight container and let freeze another hour or so to firm up before serving. Freeze for up to three weeks.

SERVING SIZE: ½ cup   CALORIES: 280   TOTAL FAT: 9 g   CARBS: 46 g   DIETARY FIBER: 7 g   PROTEIN: 6 g

MAI TAI SORBET

Whether in the heat of the summer or the gloom of winter, this exotically flavored sorbet delivers so much delicious refreshment—fat-free! I like to serve it with some fresh pineapple chunks or slices of mango, but you could make a festive cocktail "float" by putting a scoop into a Collins glass, adding a bit more rum, and finishing with a splash of soda water or ginger beer. **MAKES FOUR ½-CUP SERVINGS**

¼ c. sugar

¼ c. water

¼ c. pineapple juice

¼ c. passion fruit puree

¼ c. orange juice

½ c. guava nectar

6 Tbsp. dark rum

1 Tbsp. lime juice

4 tsp. grenadine

In a large saucepan, make a simple syrup by boiling the sugar and water together for 2 minutes. Take the syrup from the heat and stir in the pineapple juice, passion fruit puree, orange juice, guava nectar, rum, lime juice, and grenadine. Chill the mixture if it's still slightly warm and then freeze in an ice-cream maker according to the manufacturer's instructions.

SERVING SIZE: ½ cup   **CALORIES:** 170   **TOTAL FAT:** 0 g   **CARBS:** 29 g   **DIETARY FIBER:** 2 g
PROTEIN: 0 g

GINGERBREAD TUILE with VANILLA ICE CREAM and BANANAS FOSTER SAUCE

Tuiles are very thin, flat French cookies that are delicious as wafers but also have the delightful ability to be molded into shapes while they're still warm. I like to mold these spice-scented cookies into a delicate bowl and then fill with ice cream and some bananas in a warm, caramelly sauce. **MAKES 8 SERVINGS**

½ tsp. ground ginger

¼ tsp. cinnamon

Pinch cloves

Pinch nutmeg

¼ c. butter

½ c. plus 2 Tbsp. powdered sugar

2 Tbsp. molasses

2 egg whites

½ c. plus 2 Tbsp. all-purpose flour

1 recipe Bananas Foster Sauce (recipe follows)

1 pint vanilla ice cream

Heat the oven to 350°F. Whisk the ginger, cinnamon, cloves, and nutmeg together in a small bowl and set aside.

In a standing mixer fitted with a paddle attachment, cream together the butter and sugar. Add the molasses and egg whites and continue to mix for 1 minute (scraping down the sides of the bowl with a rubber spatula). Next, add the flour and spices and beat until smooth.

MAKE A STENCIL: Trace a 4-inch (diameter) circle on a thin plastic lid (such as a cottage cheese or yogurt container). Using a sharp knife or razor blade, carefully cut out the circle. Place stencil on a silicone baking mat and spread about 3 tablespoons of the batter over the circle using an offset spatula. Remove stencil and repeat this process eight times. (You may need to use more than one baking mat.)

Bake the tuiles for 10 minutes or until slightly brown around the edges. Remove from oven and using a thin spatula, quickly place each circle over the back of a 4-ounce (standard) muffin tin or an upturned ramekin to create a bowl shape.

BANANAS FOSTER SAUCE

MAKES ABOUT 1¼ CUPS

1 c. pineapple juice

½ c. dark rum

2 Tbsp. butter

½ tsp. cinnamon

¼ c. brown sugar

1 tsp. cornstarch

1 tsp. water

3 bananas, sliced at an angle

Put the pineapple juice, rum, butter, cinnamon, and brown sugar in a small saucepan and bring to a boil, stirring until smooth.

In a separate small bowl, whisk together the cornstarch and water, making a slurry. Add the slurry to the boiling sauce, whisking constantly, and continue to cook for 1 minute. Remove from heat and reserve until ready to serve. When ready to serve, reheat sauce and simmer until syrupy. Add the sliced bananas and gently toss to coat.

Arrange a tuile cup on a plate, fill with 2 ounces of vanilla ice cream, and spoon on the Bananas Foster Sauce. Serve immediately.

SERVING SIZE: 1 tuile with 2 oz. ice cream and 1 tablespoon sauce   **CALORIES:** 310
TOTAL FAT: 11 g   **CARBS:** 46 g   **DIETARY FIBER:** 1 g   **PROTEIN:** 3 g

CHOCOLATE-DIPPED PIZZELLES with HONEY LAVENDER GELATO

This is a dessert for a special occasion. It requires a bit of planning, but it sure delivers as a treat. To make the pizzelles, you'll need a pizzelle iron; both stove-top and electric models are available. The batter will keep up to 6 days in the refrigerator or 1 month in the freezer, so if you don't want to bake off all 12 pizzelles at once, you can save some for later. And it's okay to use store-bought ice cream or gelato, too. I confess that at home I don't always serve homemade! **MAKES 12 PIZZELLES**

1 egg

1 egg white

⅓ c. sugar

¼ c. melted unsalted butter

1 tsp. vanilla extract

¾ c. plus 1 tsp. unbleached all-purpose flour

1 tsp. baking powder

4 oz. melted chocolate

1 recipe Honey Lavender Gelato (recipe follows)

In a medium bowl, whisk together the egg, egg white, and sugar. Add the melted butter and vanilla extract and stir to blend. In a separate bowl, sift the flour and baking powder together and then add to the wet ingredients and whisk until smooth.

Heat a pizzelle iron, pour 1 tablespoon of batter on the iron, and cook according to manufacturer's instructions. Once cooked and still warm, gently bend the pizzelle into desired shape (such as a cone or bowl).

Once the pizzelles are cool, dip the top of each one into the melted chocolate. Let sit at room temperate until set and ready to use. When ready to serve, scoop 2 ounces of the gelato (or an ice cream of your choice) into each pizzelle cup and serve immediately.

SERVING SIZE: 1 pizzelle and 2 oz. of gelato   **CALORIES:** 270   **TOTAL FAT:** 16 g   **CARBS:** 30 g   **DIETARY FIBER:** 1 g   **PROTEIN:** 5 g

HONEY LAVENDER GELATO

MAKES 4 CUPS (SIXTEEN 2-OZ. SERVINGS)

2¼ c. whole milk

2 Tbsp. dried lavender

¼ c. honey

¾ c. heavy cream

5 egg yolks

¼ c. sugar

In a saucepan, combine the milk, lavender, honey, and cream and bring to a gentle simmer. Remove from the heat and leave to steep for 45 minutes.

In a bowl, whisk together the yolks and sugar until well blended and then slowly pour in the warm milk, whisking constantly. Strain the mixture to remove the lavender and freeze in an ice-cream maker according to manufacturer's instructions.

SERVING SIZE: 2 oz.   **CALORIES:** 80   **TOTAL FAT:** 3 g   **CARBS:** 9 g   **DIETARY FIBER:** 0 g   **PROTEIN:** 2 g

COCONUT SORBET with SAUTÉED PLUMS

I think plums are an overlooked fruit in the pastry repertoire. You don't see a lot of desserts using plums, yet they are so perfect, especially when you cook them. A raw plum is delicious, of course, but the fruit develops a whole new character when cooked—slightly spicy, perfumed, and with a juicy tenderness that's just right to spoon over some sorbet … or the pound cake on page 161. **SERVES 12**

SORBET

1 c. water

1 c. granulated sugar

4 c. lite coconut milk

½ c. fresh lime juice

½ c. coconut rum

PLUMS

6 plums, pit removed and sliced into ¼-inch wedges

¼ c. sugar

2 Tbsp. honey

3 star anise

Pinch cinnamon

Pinch Chinese 5-spice powder

1 vanilla bean, split lengthwise, seeds scraped out and reserved

MAKE THE SORBET: Combine the water and sugar in a saucepan and bring to a boil. Add the coconut milk, lime juice, and coconut rum to the sugar-water mixture. Freeze in an ice-cream maker following the manufacturer's instructions.

MAKE THE PLUMS: Put all ingredients in a medium sauté pan and cook over medium heat until plums are tender, glazed, and fragrant, about 2 minutes. Remove the anise stars and serve the plums slightly warm over a scoop of coconut sorbet.

SERVING SIZE: ½ of a plum and 2 oz. of gelato   **CALORIES:** 320   **TOTAL FAT:** 19 g   **CARBS:** 33 g   **DIETARY FIBER:** 2 g   **PROTEIN:** 2 g

PASSION FRUIT SOUFFLÉ GLACÉ

A baked soufflé rises above the rim of the soufflé dish on its own in the heat of the oven. But a frozen or chilled soufflé doesn't get baked, so you need to create the dramatic height by using a "collar." You tuck a wide strip of parchment around the inside of the dish so that it stands above the rim and will contain your soufflé mixture. Once the soufflé has set, from the gelatin and by being frozen, you can remove the collar and serve. **MAKES 8**

¼ c. water, for blooming gelatin

2½ tsp. powdered gelatin

½ c. passion fruit puree

¼ c. fat-free vanilla yogurt

¼ c. low-fat buttermilk

1 tsp. vanilla extract

½ c. sugar

¼ c. nonfat milk

4 egg whites

Cut eight 3-inch x 2-inch strips of parchment and spray one side lightly with nonstick cooking spray. Arrange one strip inside each ramekin (sprayed side in) so that it stands up around the inside rim like a collar. Set aside.

Put the water in a small bowl, sprinkle the gelatin over it, and leave until the gelatin has expanded and softened, called "blooming." Set aside.

In a mixing bowl, whip together the passion fruit puree, yogurt, buttermilk, vanilla, and half of the sugar. Set aside.

Heat a saucepan over medium heat, add the milk and gelatin and any water that wasn't absorbed and heat to a bare simmer, stirring until the gelatin has dissolved.

Stir the milk into the puree-yogurt mixture and set aside.

In a stand mixer fitted with a whip attachment, whip the egg whites to medium peaks. Add the remaining sugar and continue to mix until stiff peaks form. Fold the whipped egg whites into the puree mixture. Carefully spoon about ¾-cup into each prepared ramekin. Freeze for 4 hours or until ready to serve.

When ready to serve, gently remove the collars from the ramekins and serve right away.

SERVING SIZE: 1 ramekin **CALORIES:** 80 **TOTAL FAT:** 0 g **CARBS:** 16 g **DIETARY FIBER:** 1 g **PROTEIN:** 4 g

MIXED BERRY TORTE

This dessert makes me think of the type of rustic dessert you might see in a European bakeshop, freshly baked, full of seasonal fruit and not too sweet. The walnuts in this recipe add not only crunch but also a big boost of nutrients, as they are high in omega-3s as well as antioxidants. **MAKES 16 SERVINGS**

1 c. unbleached all-purpose flour

1 tsp. baking powder

Pinch of salt

2 Tbsp. unsalted butter, softened at room temperature

2 Tbsp. applesauce

1 c. sugar

3 egg whites

1 tsp. vanilla extract

3 oz. low-fat buttermilk

2 c. mixed berries (raspberries, blueberries, blackberries, etc.)

¼ c. ground walnuts or pecans

Heat the oven to 350°F and spray a 9-inch springform pan with nonstick cooking spray. Line the base with a circle of parchment and spray again. Set aside.

In a small bowl, sift together the flour, baking powder, and salt and set aside.

In a stand mixer fitted with a paddle attachment, cream the softened butter and applesauce together and then add the sugar. Next, add the egg whites and vanilla and mix until smooth. Start adding the flour mixture, alternating with the buttermilk, until both are incorporated and the batter is smooth (but be careful not to overmix).

Spread the berries over the bottom of the prepared springform pan, pour the batter over the top, and smooth off the top with an offset spatula. Sprinkle the nuts evenly over the top. Bake for 30 minutes or until set and golden brown. Remove from oven and let cool at room temperature. Cut into 16 servings.

SERVING SIZE: 1 slice (1/16 of cake) **CALORIES:** 80 **TOTAL FAT:** 4 g **CARBS:** 9 g
DIETARY FIBER: 1 g **PROTEIN:** 2 g

TIRAMISU TORTE

This is a beautiful dessert to serve for a dinner party because by its very nature, it must be made ahead by at least a day. So when it's time for the party, all you need to do is remove the torte from the freezer about 30 minutes before you're ready to serve. The flavors of dark chocolate, coffee, and slightly bitter cocoa make this both indulgent and sophisticated. I like to use real mascarpone and heavy cream for a more delectable torte, cutting back on high-fat ingredients only where it won't be noticed.

MAKE ONE 9-INCH TORTE, 16 SERVINGS

TORTE

4 eggs, separated

¾ c. sugar

6 oz. Neufchâtel cheese, softened

6 oz. mascarpone cheese

1 tsp. vanilla extract

1½ c. heavy cream

½ c. strong brewed or instant coffee

¼ c. Amaretto liqueur

20 ladyfingers

GANACHE TOPPING

¾ c. chopped 64 percent dark chocolate

½ c. half-and-half

¼ c. nonfat milk

Spray a 9-inch springform pan with nonstick cooking spray and then line the base with a circle of parchment and spray again.

In a stand mixer fitted with a whip attachment, combine the egg yolks and ½ cup of the sugar and whip for 2 minutes or until thick and pale yellow. Add the softened Neufchâtel cheese, mascarpone, and vanilla extract and continue to whip until combined and smooth. Transfer the yolk-cheese mixture to another medium bowl and set aside.

Using the same mixing bowl, whip the heavy cream to medium peaks and gently fold into the yolk-cheese base using a rubber spatula.

Wash the mixer bowl, dry completely, and then whip the egg whites to soft peaks. Slowly pour in the remaining ¼ cup of sugar and continue to whip until medium peaks form. Fold the whipped egg whites into the yolk-cheese base using a rubber spatula. Cover and refrigerate the mousse until you're ready to assemble the torte.

(CONTINUED)

Combine the coffee and Amaretto in a squeeze bottle or measuring cup with a pour spout and set aside.

Place 10 ladyfingers in the bottom of the springform pan as closely together as possible. (You may have to cut the ladyfingers to fit.) Moisten the ladyfingers with coffee-amaretto until they're nicely saturated, using about half of the liquid.

Pour half of the mousse over the ladyfingers and spread evenly with a palette knife. Place remaining ladyfingers over the mousse in the opposite direction of the bottom layer of ladyfingers. Moisten them with the remaining coffee mixture. Pour the remaining mousse over the top and smooth the surface. Refrigerate for 30 minutes.

While the torte is chilling, make the ganache. Put the chopped chocolate in a bowl. In a saucepan, bring the half-and-half and milk to a simmer. Remove from the heat and pour over chocolate in a bowl. Let sit for 1 minute and then stir until smooth and completely melted. Let the ganache cool to room temperature.

When cool, pour the ganache over the top of the mousse and move the springform pan in a circular motion so that the ganache flows to cover the whole surface of the torte. (Do not use any tool to smooth the surface if you can help it; this will create streaks.)

Place the torte in the freezer for 8 hours until firm. Slice the torte into 16 slices when still frozen. When you're ready to serve, remove from the freezer and let sit at room temperature for about 30 minutes until partially softened.

SERVING SIZE: 1 slice (¹⁄₁₆ of cake) **CALORIES:** 268 **TOTAL FAT:** 20 g **CARBS:** 17 g
DIETARY FIBER: .5 g **PROTEIN:** 5 g

VANILLA CHEESECAKE with CINNAMON APPLE COMPOTE and APPLE CHIPS

At Miraval, I like to serve this dessert as a cheesecake "parfait" by piping the creamy filling into pretty glasses and garnishing with the compote and delicate apple chips. But you could keep things simpler by swirling the cooled compote through the filling and then scooping it into little bowls. I love desserts that can be plain or fancy, as you like.

MAKES 16

VANILLA CHEESECAKE

1½ c. Neufchâtel cheese

3 c. pureed cottage cheese

2 Tbsp. sugar

8 sheets gelatin (8 tsp. powdered gelatin)

1½ c. nonfat milk

1 Tbsp. vanilla extract

CINNAMON APPLE COMPOTE

1 tsp. butter

2 c. medium-diced Granny Smith apple

¼ c. sugar

½ tsp. cinnamon

MAKE THE CHEESECAKE: In a stand mixer fitted with a paddle attachment, cream the Neufchâtel cheese and pureed cottage cheese together and then add the sugar and mix until nicely blended.

Sprinkle the gelatin over ½-cup cold water in a small bowl to soften and "bloom" it. Set aside for 2 minutes.

In a saucepan, heat the milk and add the softened gelatin. Cook for 30 seconds, stirring constantly until dissolved. Pour the warm milk into the cream-cheese mixture and mix until smooth. Add the vanilla extract and mix to blend.

Transfer the cheesecake batter to a container, cover, and refrigerate for 4 hours, until it has firmed up.

MAKE THE APPLE COMPOTE: In a sauté pan, heat the butter over medium heat until melted and then add the apples, sugar, and cinnamon. Cook for 2 minutes or until the apples have softened slightly and started to caramelized. Cool to room temperature.

APPLE CHIPS

**1 Granny Smith apple,
sliced very thin, peel on**

1 Tbsp. powdered sugar

MAKE THE APPLE CHIPS: Heat the oven to 200°F. Place the thinly sliced apples on a nonstick baking mat (such as a Silpat) and sprinkle the powdered sugar over the top. Bake for 40 to 50 minutes or until the apple slices are crisp. You can test the crispness by removing one of the apple slices from the oven and cooling for 2 minutes.

ASSEMBLE THE DESSERT: Pipe the set cheesecake batter into a pretty glass and top with a spoonful of apple compote and a crisp apple chip.

CALORIES: 280 **TOTAL FAT:** 4.5 g **CARBS:** 54 g **DIETARY FIBER:** 1 g **PROTEIN:** 9 g

ORANGE MASCARPONE CHEESECAKE

One of my tricks in the Miraval pastry kitchen is to use applesauce in place of a fat, such as butter. In this recipe, I'm using it in the graham-cracker crust, which is such a key component of a classic cheesecake but is usually very buttery. In my version, you get the buttery flavor without all the fat. **MAKES ONE 9-INCH CHEESECAKE, 16 SERVINGS**

2 c. graham-cracker crumbs

1 Tbsp. unsalted butter, melted

1 Tbsp. applesauce

3 c. low-fat cottage cheese, blended until smooth

½ c. low-fat cream cheese, softened at room temperature

1 c. mascarpone cheese, softened at room temperature

2 c. raw cane sugar

1 tsp. finely grated orange zest

¼ c. cold water (to soften gelatin)

5 tsp. powdered gelatin

1¼ c. fresh orange juice

1 Tbsp. Grand Marnier liqueur

Mixed fresh berries, for serving

Heat the oven to 350°F. Prepare a 9-inch springform pan with parchment paper and nonstick cooking spray.

Combine the graham-cracker crumbs, melted butter, and applesauce in a small bowl and mix until moist crumbs form. Press the crust into the prepared springform pan. Bake for 10 minutes until golden brown. Cool the crust to room temperature and set aside.

In a mixer fitted with a paddle attachment, cream the pureed cottage cheese, cream cheese, and mascarpone together until smooth. Add the sugar and zest and beat to blend.

In a small bowl, combine ¼-cup cold water and the gelatin and let sit for 2 minutes, until softened. In a small saucepan, heat the orange juice until it comes to a simmer, add the gelatin, and stir until dissolved. Add the gelatin-juice mixture and the Grand Marnier to the cheesecake batter and mix until smooth. Pour the batter into the prepared crust and refrigerate for at least 8 hours, until set. Cut the cheesecake into 16 slices. Serve with fresh berries.

SERVING SIZE: 1 slice (¹⁄₁₆ of cake)   **CALORIES:** 320   **TOTAL FAT:** 16 g   **CARBS:** 36 g
DIETARY FIBER: 0 g   **PROTEIN:** 9 g

FRANGELICO CRÈME CARAMEL

Crème caramel is one of those desserts that you often see on restaurant menus that is really quite easy to make at home. The first step—making caramel—takes a bit of concentration in order to get the caramel just the right degree of doneness, but the rest of the dish is simple and so nice to make for dinner parties. **MAKES 6 SERVINGS**

1 c. granulated sugar

¼ c. water

1 c. nonfat milk

½ c. 2 percent milk

3 Tbsp. half-and-half

1 vanilla bean, split, seeds scraped out with tip of a knife and reserved

4 large egg whites

1 large egg

¼ c. raw cane sugar

1 Tbsp. Frangelico liqueur

¼ tsp. almond extract

Heat the oven to 325°F. Put the granulated sugar and water in a saucepan and cook over medium heat, stirring constantly until the sugar is dissolved. Bring to a boil and cook until sugar caramelizes to an amber color. Remove from the heat and pour into six lightly greased 4-ounce ramekins. (Take care, because the caramel is very hot.) Arrange the ramekins in a large roasting pan and fill with hot water until it comes halfway up the sides of the ramekins. Set aside.

Place the nonfat milk, 2 percent milk, half-and-half, and the vanilla bean and seeds in a saucepan and bring to a simmer over low heat. Remove from the heat, cover, and leave to steep for at least 30 minutes. Return the pan to the stove and bring the mixture back to a gentle boil.

Meanwhile, combine the egg whites, eggs, cane sugar, Frangelico, and almond extract in a bowl. Temper the egg mixture by whisking a little of the hot milk into the egg mixture. Once that's blended, you can whisk in the rest of the hot milk. Strain the mixture through a fine mesh sieve and pour it into the prepared ramekins. Bake in the prepared water bath for 1 hour or until set but still with a slight jiggle in the center. Remove from the water bath and chill for at least 4 hours, preferably overnight.

To serve, run a hot knife around the inside edge of the ramekins and invert onto a plate.

SERVING SIZE: 1 ramekin **CALORIES:** 230 **TOTAL FAT:** 2 g **CARBS:** 46 g **DIETARY FIBER:** 0 g **PROTEIN:** 6 g

CHOCOLATE CRÈME BRÛLÉE

I love to watch the guests at Miraval as they start to eat my crème brûlée to see the look of delight when they crack through the crisp caramel topping and find the creamy custard below. Creating that crisp topping at home does require a special tool, a small kitchen blowtorch, which you can find at any kitchen equipment shop or online. It's simple to use—and quite fun—and will allow you to gently burn the sugar topping without overcooking the custard. **MAKES 8**

2 c. 2 percent milk

½ c. nonfat milk

1 c. nonfat dry powdered milk

⅓ c. plus 3½ tsp. granulated sugar

6 egg yolks

¾ c. chopped semi-sweet chocolate

¼ c. chocolate sauce (recipe follows)

Heat the oven to 325°F. Spray eight 4-ounce ramekins with nonstick cooking spray. Arrange them in a roasting pan and add hot water to come halfway up the ramekins.

Combine the 2 percent, nonfat, and powdered milks and ⅓ cup of the sugar in a saucepan and heat until hot.

Combine the yolks, 2 tsp. sugar, chopped chocolate, and chocolate sauce in a bowl. Slowly whisk the hot milk into the yolk mixture. Strain and pour into ramekins. Bake in the water bath for 40 minutes, until set but still slightly jiggly in the center. Cool for 4 hours in the refrigerator and then brûlée when ready to serve.

TO BRÛLÉE: Sprinkle the remaining 1½ teaspoons granulated sugar in an even layer over the surface of each crème brûlée. Using a kitchen blowtorch, carefully caramelize the sugar until nicely melted and slightly burnt.

SERVING SIZE: 1 ramekin **CALORIES:** 290 **TOTAL FAT:** 10 g **CARBS:** 42 g **DIETARY FIBER:** 2 g **PROTEIN:** 12 g

CHOCOLATE SAUCE

MAKES 2 CUPS

¾ c. unsweetened cocoa powder

½ c. granulated sugar

½ c. boiling water

½ c. maple syrup

½ Tbsp. vanilla extract

In a medium-sized bowl, combine cocoa powder and sugar. Slowly add the boiling water while whisking constantly. Add in maple syrup and vanilla extract and whisk until smooth. Strain through a fine mesh strainer and transfer to a container. Refrigerate for at least 2 hours before serving. Keep refrigerated for up to two weeks or freeze for up to 1 month.

SERVING SIZE: 2 tablespoons or 1 fluid ounce   **CALORIES:** 50   **TOTAL FAT:** 0.5 g
CARBS: 11 g   **DIETARY FIBER:** 0 g   **PROTEIN:** 3 g

LEMON PANNA COTTA with BLACKBERRY COMPOTE

Panna cotta is an Italian dessert that is like a custard except that it has no eggs in it. The texture comes from gelatin, and there's no need to cook it. I love the feel of panna cotta, which is both creamy but quite light. It's a lovely dessert for entertaining because you make the panna cottas a day ahead to give them time to set. To serve, you just dress up with some fruit or a sauce. My favorite is a blackberry compote, but any berry would be delicious with the delicate lemon flavor of the dessert. **MAKES 6 SERVINGS**

2 c. 2 percent milk

¼ c. heavy cream

¼ c. granulated sugar

1 vanilla bean, split lengthwise, seeds scraped and reserved

4 tsp. gelatin

¼ c. water

¼ tsp. lemon extract (not imitation)

1 recipe Blackberry Compote (recipe follows)

Heat the milk, cream, sugar, and vanilla bean and seeds together in a saucepan. Sprinkle the gelatin over ¼ cup of water and let bloom for 2 minutes.

Add the bloomed gelatin to the milk mixture and stir until melted. Remove from the heat. Strain the mixture through a fine mesh sieve to remove any bits of undissolved gelatin and then stir in the lemon extract. Pour into six 4-ounce glasses (filling a little over ¾ of the way) and refrigerate for 4 hours.

When chilled, pour about 3 tablespoons of the cooled blackberry compote over the panna cotta and serve.

SERVING SIZE: 1 four-ounce glass   **CALORIES:** 160   **TOTAL FAT:** 5 g   **CARBS:** 23 g
DIETARY FIBER: 2 g   **PROTEIN:** 5 g

BLACKBERRY COMPOTE

MAKES 6 SERVINGS

1½ tsp. cornstarch

1½ tsp. water

1½ c. blackberries (Frozen is fine.)

3 Tbsp. granulated sugar

1 tsp. fresh lemon juice

Put the cornstarch and water in a small bowl or cup and mix with your finger to make a smooth paste. This is called a slurry.

Put the blackberries, sugar, and lemon juice in a small saucepan and bring to a boil. (The berries should be giving off some juices.) When the sauce is boiling, stir in the slurry, boil for a few more seconds, and then remove from the heat. Serve chilled.

SERVING SIZE: ¼ cup   **CALORIES:** 45   **TOTAL FAT:** 0 g   **CARBS:** 11 g   **DIETARY FIBER:** 2 g   **PROTEIN:** 1 g

CINNAMON-RAISIN BOURBON BREAD PUDDING

A touch of "southern comfort" comes to Miraval in this bourbon-scented homey dessert. Bread puddings are a terrific way to use up leftover bread, and just about any type of bread will work fine, provided it doesn't contain ingredients like onions or olives. Just make sure you give the bread enough time to soak up the custard; denser breads may take a bit longer than the 15 minutes in the recipe. **SERVES 16**

⅓ c. raisins

3 Tbsp. unsalted butter, melted

7 whole eggs

3⅓ c. 2 percent milk

1¼ c. granulated sugar, more for sprinkling

1 tsp. cinnamon, more for sprinkling

1 tsp. pure vanilla extract

2 Tbsp. bourbon

5 c. cubed white or wheat bread

Heat the oven to 350°F and spray an 8-inch x 8-inch baking dish with nonstick spray. Sprinkle half of the raisins over the bottom of the pan and set aside.

Combine the melted butter, eggs, milk, sugar, cinnamon, vanilla, and bourbon together in a large bowl and whisk until smooth. Add the bread and let soak for 15 minutes or until it has completely absorbed the custard. Pour bread pudding into pan and sprinkle with the remaining raisins.

Finish with a little cinnamon and sugar if desired. Bake for 20 minutes or until the pudding is set and light golden brown.

SERVING SIZE: 1⁄16 of cake or a 2-inch x 2-inch slice   **CALORIES:** 180   **TOTAL FAT:** 6 g
CARBS: 26 g   **DIETARY FIBER:** 1 g   **PROTEIN:** 6 g

CHOCOLATE PEANUT BUTTER TAMALES

I like desserts that not only taste good but that also make you smile because they're a clever twist on something familiar. These tamales do both. I use the cornmeal flour called masa harina, which is the main ingredient in traditional savory tamales, but I sweeten and flavor them with some peanut butter. The chocolate chips melt when you steam the tamales, providing a gooey-chocolaty filling. That will also make you smile!

SERVES 12

2 c. masa harina

2 Tbsp. oil

1 tsp. baking powder

6 Tbsp. organic peanut butter

1 c. water

½ c. semisweet chocolate chips

12 corn husks, soaked in water for 15 minutes

In a small bowl combine the masa, oil, baking powder, peanut butter, and water. Mix the batter until smooth and moist. Fold in the chocolate chips, and place a ½ cup of masa mixture in a corn husk. Use the corn husk to roll the masa up into a roll. Make sure the batter is completely covered by the husk. Steam tamales for 20 minutes, until slightly firm.

SERVING SIZE: 1 tamale **CALORIES:** 210 **TOTAL FAT:** 10 g **CARBS:** 29 g **DIETARY FIBER:** 3 g **PROTEIN:** 5 g

MERINGUE TARTLETS: CLASSIC FRUIT and LEMON CURD

An individual tart, glistening with golden lemon curd or bright with artfully arranged fresh fruit, is a beautiful and sophisticated dessert. I learned to make French tarts in cooking school, and I still enjoy making them. But now my tarts have the Miraval touch because instead of a standard pastry crust, I make a meringue crust. It's delicious and virtually fat-free. If you would like to make your own pastry crust, I've included a recipe for an easy graham-cracker crust on page 189. **MAKES 16 INDIVIDUAL TARTS**

TART SHELLS

3 egg whites

¼ tsp. cream of tartar (optional; use if your environment is humid)

¾ c. fine sugar (sometimes called "Baker's Sugar")

½ tsp. vanilla extract

Lemon Curd (recipe follows) or Low-Fat Pastry Cream (recipe follows)

Heat the oven to 225°F. In a stand mixer fitted with a whip attachment, beat egg whites (and cream of tartar, if using) until almost at soft peak. Slowly start to add in the sugar 2 tablespoons at a time. Continue to beat until stiff peaks form and whites are smooth, not grainy. Whisk in vanilla.

With a piping bag, or gallon zip-top bag (with corner cut off), pipe meringue into the bottom of a greased 4-inch wide ramekin in a swirling motion (just enough to cover the bottom). Then start to build up the sides to form a rim. TIP: You can use a star tip to create a more elaborate design.

Bake for about 1 to 1½ hours or until firm and an inserted toothpick comes out clean. Turn off oven and let the tarts dry in the oven until cool and crisp. Fill with desired filling right before serving.

FOR LEMON CURD TARTS: Fill with about 3 tablespoons chilled lemon curd right before serving.

FOR CLASSIC FRUIT TARTS: Fill each tart with 3 tablespoons pastry cream. Decorate the top with fresh fruit (such as blueberries, raspberries, strawberries, orange segments, kiwi slices, or peach slices).

SERVING SIZE: 1 tart **CALORIES:** 280 **TOTAL FAT:** 8 g **CARBS:** 49 g **DIETARY FIBER:** 0 g **PROTEIN:** 4 g

LEMON CURD

MAKES ABOUT 3 CUPS, ENOUGH FOR 16 INDIVIDUAL TARTS

1 c. water

1 c. lemon juice

5 yolks

6 Tbsp. cornstarch

1½ c. sugar

In a saucepan, combine all ingredients and whisk until smooth. Place the pan over medium heat and stir constantly until the curd thickens and bubbles. Strain through a fine mesh strainer and transfer to a container. Refrigerate for 2 hours or until thoroughly chilled.

SERVING SIZE: ¼ cup **CALORIES:** 110 **TOTAL FAT:** 1.5 g **CARBS:** 23 g **DIETARY FIBER:** 0 g **PROTEIN:** 1 g

EASY GRAHAM TART CRUST

MAKES 4 SERVINGS

¼ c. graham-cracker crumbs

4 Tbsp. butter, melted

1 Tbsp. applesauce

3 Tbsp. sugar

In a medium bowl, combine all four ingredients together until the mixture is slightly moist and holds together. Evenly divide the crust among four ¾-inch x ¾-inch tart pans, and press firmly until matted and firm. Bake at 350°F for 12 minutes or until lightly golden brown. Remove from oven, and let cool to room temperature before attempting to unmold. Fill with your desired filling.

SERVING SIZE: 1 tart shell **CALORIES:** 273 **TOTAL FAT:** 14 g **CARBS:** 34 g **DIETARY FIBER:** 1 g **PROTEIN:** 2 g

LOW-FAT PASTRY CREAM

MAKES 4 CUPS, ENOUGH FOR 20 INDIVIDUAL TARTS

⅓ c. cornstarch

2 large egg yolks

4 c. nonfat milk, divided

¾ c. raw cane sugar

1 vanilla bean, split in half lengthwise, seeds scraped out

In a mixing bowl, combine the cornstarch, egg yolks, and ¼ cup of the milk. Combine the remaining milk, the sugar, and vanilla in a medium saucepan and heat over medium-high heat, stirring to dissolve the sugar, until the mixture comes to a simmer.

Slowly whisk the hot milk into the egg mixture, whisking constantly. Return the egg mixture to the saucepan and cook over medium heat, stirring constantly, until the pastry cream reaches a thick consistency, about 5 minutes. Strain through a fine mesh strainer.

Pour the pastry cream into a bowl. Press a piece of plastic wrap on the surface of the cream and chill for at least 1 hour for pastry cream to thicken.

SERVING SIZE: ¼ cup   **CALORIES:** 70   **TOTAL FAT:** 1.5 g   **CARBS:** 12 g   **DIETARY FIBER:** 0 g **PROTEIN:** 2 g

Afterword

While reviewing the final manuscript for this cookbook, we stepped back to take stock of our work on the project. We were pleased to have shared so many of our favorite recipes, tips, and ideas—the elements that make up the cooking that we enjoy in the Miraval kitchens and in our own at home.

We also realized that what we really shared with readers is our philosophy on food and the role it plays in our lives. After spending many years cooking for others, we've come to believe that food is much more than just calories or nutrients. The act of cooking and eating delicious, healthful food is a way to get in touch with the seasons, the land, and its bounty of fresh ingredients. Just as important, cooking is a way to connect with ourselves, our friends, and our family. Sitting down together for a nutritious meal is a way to step out of the fast-paced world and nourish our body, mind, and spirit. It's a simple act that is incredibly powerful.

We hope that as you explore the book and do your own cooking from it, we'll be helping you find your own power, too.

— Justin and Kim

Acknowledgments

We would like to thank Michael Tompkins, Carol Stratford, Leeann Ray, Junelle Lupiani, Kris Wright, J.D. Martin, Tyler Brady, and the Miraval Culinary Team for all their hard work, support, and dedication.

Additionally, special thanks to Martha Holmberg, for helping to bring this book to fruition with her ability to capture our food, and us, with her writing style.

Conversion Charts

STANDARD CUP	FINE POWDER (e.g., flour)	GRAIN (e.g., rice)	GRANULAR (e.g., sugar)	LIQUID SOLIDS (e.g., butter)	LIQUID (e.g., milk)
1	140 g	150 g	190 g	200 g	240 ml
¾	105 g	113 g	143 g	150 g	180 ml
⅔	93 g	100 g	125 g	133 g	160 ml
½	70 g	75 g	95 g	100 g	120 ml
⅓	47 g	50 g	63 g	67 g	80 ml
¼	35 g	38 g	48 g	50 g	60 ml
⅛	18 g	19 g	24 g	25 g	30 ml

USEFUL EQUIVALENTS FOR LIQUID INGREDIENTS BY VOLUME

¼ tsp				1 ml	
½ tsp				2 ml	
1 tsp				5 ml	
3 tsp	1 tbsp		½ fl oz	15 ml	
	2 tbsp	⅛ cup	1 fl oz	30 ml	
	4 tbsp	¼ cup	2 fl oz	60 ml	
	5⅓ tbsp	⅓ cup	3 fl oz	80 ml	
	8 tbsp	½ cup	4 fl oz	120 ml	
	10⅔ tbsp	⅔ cup	5 fl oz	160 ml	
	12 tbsp	¾ cup	6 fl oz	180 ml	
	16 tbsp	1 cup	8 fl oz	240 ml	
	1 pt	2 cups	16 fl oz	480 ml	
	1 qt	4 cups	32 fl oz	960 ml	
			33 fl oz	1000 ml	1 l

USEFUL EQUIVALENTS FOR DRY INGREDIENTS BY WEIGHT
(To convert ounces to grams, multiply the number of ounces by 30.)

1 oz	1/16 lb	30 g
4 oz	¼ lb	120 g
8 oz	½ lb	240 g
12 oz	¾ lb	360 g
16 oz	1 lb	480 g

USEFUL EQUIVALENTS FOR COOKING/OVEN TEMPERATURES

Process	Fahrenheit	Celsius	Gas Mark
Freeze Water	32° F	0° C	
Room Temperature	68° F	20° C	
Boil Water	212° F	100° C	
Bake	325° F	160°	C 3
	350° F	180°	C 4
	375° F	190°	C 5
	400° F	200°	C 6
	425° F	220°	C 7
	450° F	230°	C 8
Broil			Grill

USEFUL EQUIVALENTS FOR LENGTH
(To convert inches to centimeters, multiply the number of inches by 2.5.)

1 in		2.5 cm		
6 in	½ ft		15 cm	
12 in	1 ft		30 cm	
36 in	3 ft	1 yd	90 cm	
40 in			100 cm	1 m

Index

About the Authors

JUSTIN CLINE MACY is the executive chef at Miraval Resort & Spa, where he has honed his culinary skills and expertise in spa cuisine since 1999. He enjoys exploring the nuances of diverse cultural cuisines and pushing the boundaries in his cooking by combining international flavors while staying true to spa cuisine's goal of creating a healthy, nutritious, and appetizing plate.

Justin has appeared as a guest on several national broadcast shows, including *The Oprah Winfrey Show* and *The Millionaire Matchmaker*. He has developed the "Evening with the Chef" weekend series, featuring cooking demos and wine-pairing suggestions, as well as the In-Villa Culinary Program for Miraval residential villas, which caters to private owners, celebrities, and high-profile guests. In his free time, he enjoys participating in cooking competitions such as his repeated visits to Bend, Oregon, for the Sage Brush Classic.

Justin has trained under such spa chef mentors as Chad Luethje, Bill Wavrin, and Cary Neff. He credits his career success to years of training and commitment but also to his family. The passion for all things culinary has been in his blood for generations, as both his mother and grandmother worked in various chef roles in commercial kitchens throughout Arizona.

Justin is also a contributing author of *Mindful Eating* and *Mindful Living Miraval*.

Inspired by her mother's cooking when she was a child, **KIM MACY** decided to pursue her passion for healthy, mindful cooking as a career. From the beginning, her goal has been to create timeless, classic cuisine with a healthy twist.

Kim graduated with honors from the Le Cordon Bleu Culinary Program at The Scottsdale Culinary Institute in Scottsdale, Arizona, in 2004. As part of her training, she interned at Athletes Performance in Tempe, Arizona, and then at Miraval Resort & Spa in Tucson, Arizona. Kim was asked to join the Culinary Team at Miraval on a permanent basis at the conclusion of her internship and has worked in all areas of the kitchen, including Garde Manger, Pantry, and Hotline. Soon realizing that her true passion was pastries, Kim has managed the Pastry Department at Miraval since 2007.

Kim's work has been showcased in major publications, including the *Arizona Daily Star, Arizona Foothills* magazine, and *Shape* magazine. Kim teaches two live cooking demonstrations a week for Miraval guests and has been a repeat guest chef on local morning television shows. A contributing author of *Mindful Eating* and *Mindful Living Miraval,* she has also participated in a recent segment featuring Miraval that aired on the Tennis Channel's *Fit to Hit.*

Kim is a very talented pastry chef, creating and implementing savory and decadent low-fat, low-calorie pastries, breads, desserts, and other baked goods for the enjoyment of Miraval's guests. While most of her demonstrations are focused on pastries, Kim also teaches classes on healthy soups, salads, appetizers, and entrées. These cooking demonstrations afford Kim the opportunity to interact with guests, answering their questions about techniques, providing information about gluten-free diets (among others), and allowing her to share her passion for preparing healthy, mindful cuisine at home.

The Miraval Experience

There are spas ... and then there is Miraval.

Miraval means "View of the Valley," a poignant name for this exclusive desert retreat nestled in the foothills of the Santa Catalina Mountains just north of Tucson, Arizona. And although some trips take you to places you've never been before, even to destinations that few others have ever seen, Miraval Resort & Spa offers the most inspiring getaway one can imagine—a journey unique to everyone who visits.

Consistently rated among the world's top spas and resorts by TripAdvisor and SpaFinder and publications such as *Travel+Leisure, Celebrated Living*, and *Condé Nast Traveler*, Miraval has earned its trendsetting reputation as America's destination for life betterment, where guests feel, are, and can be more.

Since its beginning in 1995, Miraval has upheld a powerfully simple vision: *Life is more meaningful and enjoyable when your physical, emotional, spiritual, social, and intellectual components are in balance.* To that end, Miraval offers more than 100 unique life-enhancing programs and activities. Guests plan their stay filled with an abundance of choices, including innovative spa treatments, self-discovery activities led by insightful well-being specialists, dynamic growth and development programs, outdoor challenges, yoga and Pilates, stress-management techniques, and nutritional counseling. All aim to help people better manage our fast-paced world and life's daily demands.

Guests from around the world relish the resort not only for its luxury, but also for the deep comfort they can find nowhere else—speaking to Miraval's authentic wish for every guest: *You won't find you anywhere else.*

www.MiravalResorts.com

We hope you enjoyed this Hay House book. If you'd like to receive our online catalog featuring additional information on Hay House books and products, or if you'd like to find out more about the Hay Foundation, please contact:

Hay House, Inc., P.O. Box 5100, Carlsbad, CA 92018-5100
(760) 431-7695 or (800) 654-5126
(760) 431-6948 (fax) or (800) 650-5115 (fax)
www.hayhouse.com® • www.hayfoundation.org

Published and distributed in Australia by: Hay House Australia Pty. Ltd.,
18/36 Ralph St., Alexandria NSW 2015 • Phone: 612-9669-4299 • Fax: 612-9669-4144 • www.hayhouse.com.au

Published and distributed in the United Kingdom by: Hay House UK, Ltd., Astley House,
33 Notting Hill Gate, London W11 3JQ • Phone: 44-20-3675-2450 • Fax: 44-20-3675-2451 • www.hayhouse.co.uk

Published and distributed in the Republic of South Africa by: Hay House SA (Pty), Ltd.,
P.O. Box 990, Witkoppen 2068 • Phone/Fax: 27-11-467-8904 • www.hayhouse.co.za

Published in India by: Hay House Publishers India, Muskaan Complex, Plot No. 3, B-2, Vasant Kunj,
New Delhi 110 070 • Phone: 91-11-4176-1620 • Fax: 91-11-4176-1630 • www.hayhouse.co.in

Distributed in Canada by: Raincoast, 9050 Shaughnessy St., Vancouver, B.C. V6P 6E5
Phone: (604) 323-7100 • Fax: (604) 323-2600 • www.raincoast.com

Take Your Soul on a Vacation

Visit www.HealYourLife.com® to regroup, recharge, and reconnect with your own magnificence.
Featuring blogs, mind-body-spirit news, and life-changing wisdom from Louise Hay and friends.
VISIT www.HealYourLife.com TODAY!

Free e-newsletters
from Hay House, the Ultimate
Resource for Inspiration